Collins

11+ Spatial Reasoning

Quick Practice Tests Ages 9-10

Faisal Nasim

Contents

ACKNOWLEDGEMENTS

The author and publisher are grateful to the copyright holders for permission to use quoted materials and images.

Every effort has been made to trace copyright holders and obtain their permission for the use of copyright material. The author and publisher will gladly receive information enabling them to rectify any error or omission in subsequent editions. All facts are correct at time of going to press.

Published by Collins
An imprint of HarperCollins*Publishers* Limited
1 London Bridge Street
London SE1 9GF

HarperCollins*Publishers*
Macken House
39/40 Mayor Street Upper
Dublin 1
D01 C9W8
Ireland

ISBN: 9781844199198

First published 2018

This edition published 2020

Previously published as Letts

10 9

© HarperCollins*Publishers* Limited 2020

British Library Cataloguing in Publication Data.

A CIP record of this book is available from the British Library.

Author and Series Editor: Faisal Nasim
Commissioning Editor: Michelle I'Anson
Editor and Project Manager: Sonia Dawkins
Cover Design: Sarah Duxbury and Kevin Robbins
Text and Page Design: Ian Wrigley
Layout and Artwork: Q2A Media
Printed in the UK, by Ashford Colour Ltd

MIX
Paper | Supporting responsible forestry
FSC™ C007454

This book contains FSC™ certified paper and other controlled sources to ensure responsible forest management.

For more information visit: www.harpercollins.co.uk/green

About this book

Familiarisation with 11+ test-style questions is a critical step in preparing your child for the 11+ selection tests. This book gives children lots of opportunities to test themselves in short, manageable bursts, helping to build confidence and improve the chance of test success.

It contains 25 tests designed to build key spatial reasoning skills.

- Each test is designed to be completed within a short amount of time. Frequent, short bursts of revision are found to be more productive than lengthier sessions.

- CEM tests often consist of a series of shorter, time-pressured sections so these practice tests will help your child become accustomed to this style of questioning.

- If your child does not complete any of the tests in the allocated time, they may need further practice in that area.

- We recommend your child uses a pencil to complete the tests, so that they can rub out the answers and try again at a later date if necessary.

- Children will need a pencil and a rubber to complete the tests and some spare paper for rough working. They will also need to be able to see a clock/watch and should have a quiet place in which to do the tests.

- Answers to every question are provided at the back of the book, with explanations given where appropriate.

- After completing the tests, children should revisit their weaker areas and attempt to improve their scores and timings.

Download a free progress chart from our website
collins.co.uk/11plus

Test 1

You have 6 minutes to complete this test.

You have 12 questions to complete within the given time.

In each question, circle the letter below the set of blocks that can be combined to make the figure on the left.

EXAMPLE

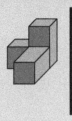 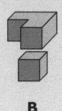 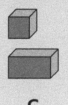 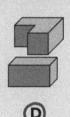

A   B   C   (D)

①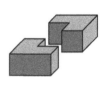

A   B   C   D

②

A   B   C   D

③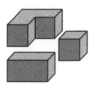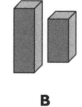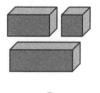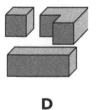

A   B   C   D

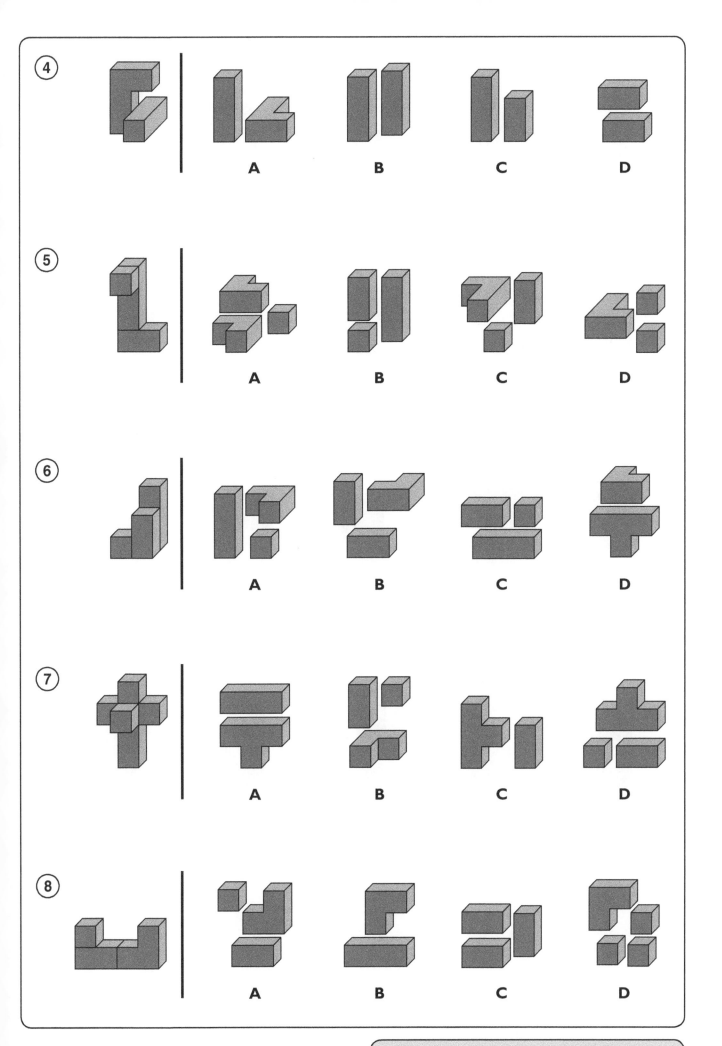

Questions continue on next page

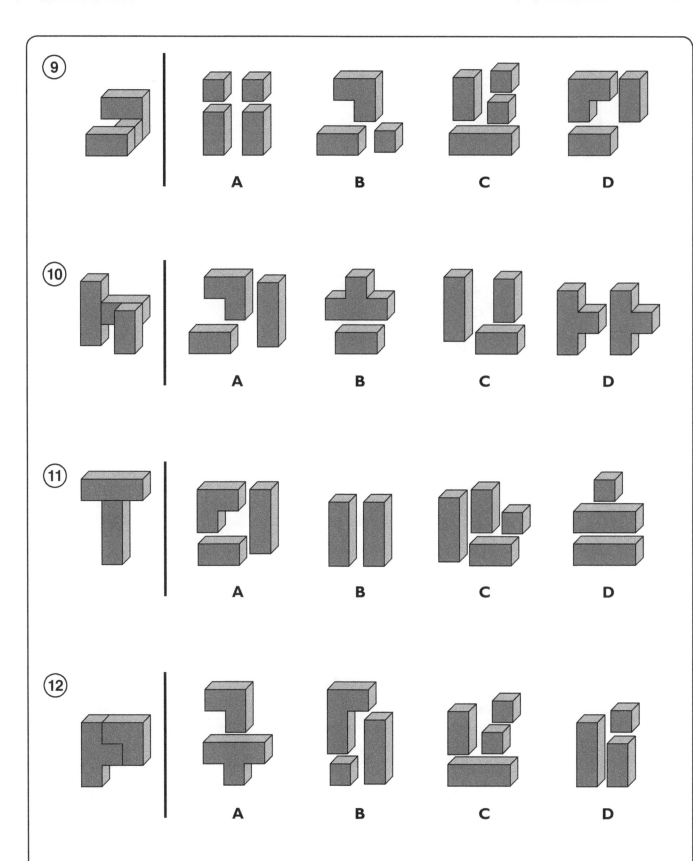

9
A B C D

10
A B C D

11
A B C D

12
A B C D

Score: .... / 12

Test 2

You have 5 minutes to complete this test.

You have 10 questions to complete within the given time.

In each question, circle the letter below the figure that can be combined with the first figure to create the shape in the grey box. The first figure must not be rotated.

EXAMPLE

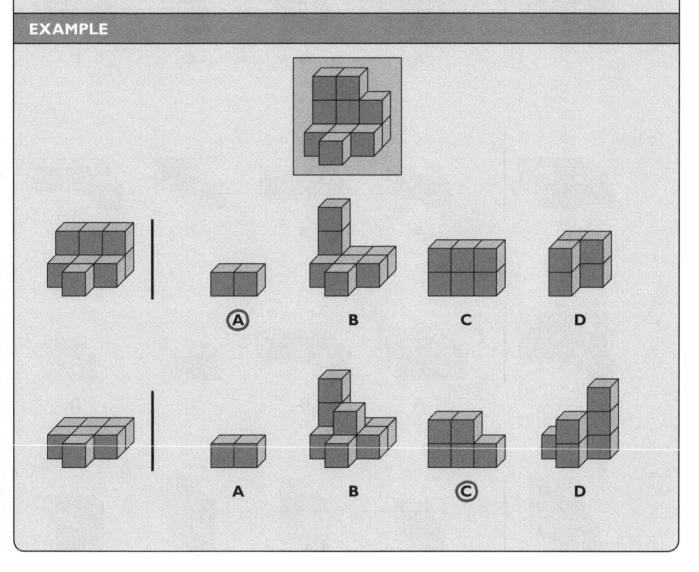

Questions start on next page

Refer to the shape in the grey box for Questions 1–5 below.

①

   A   **B**   **C**   **D**

②

   A   **B**   **C**   **D**

③

   A   **B**   **C**   **D**

④

   A   **B**   **C**   **D**

⑤

   A   **B**   **C**   **D**

Refer to the shape in the grey box for Questions 6–10 below.

(6)

A   B   C   D

(7)

A   B   C   D

(8)

A   B   C   D

(9)

A   B   C   D

(10)

A   B   C   D

Score: .... / 10

Test 3

In each question, one of the 3D figures below has been rotated to create the figure shown. Circle the letter of the figure that has been rotated.

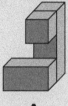

A

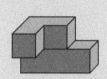

D

B

E

C

F

EXAMPLE

Ⓐ	D
B	E
C	F

1

A	D
B	E
C	F

2

A	D
B	E
C	F

10

③ 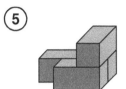   **A**   **D**

B   **E**

C   **F**

④   **A**   **D**

B   **E**

C   **F**

⑤    **A**   **D**

B   **E**

C   **F**

⑥ 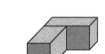   **A**   **D**

B   **E**

C   **F**

⑦   **A**   **D**

B   **E**

C   **F**

⑧ 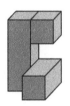   **A**   **D**

B   **E**

C   **F**

⑨   **A**   **D**

B   **E**

C   **F**

⑩    **A**   **D**

B   **E**

C   **F**

⑪    **A**   **D**

B   **E**

C   **F**

⑫   **A**   **D**

B   **E**

C   **F**

Score: .... / 12

Test 4

You have 5 minutes to complete this test.

You have 10 questions to complete within the given time.

In each question, circle the letter below the figure that shows how the left-hand figure will look when folded along the dotted line.

The fold should be made towards the dotted line, not away from it.

EXAMPLE

A   B   C   D

(A)

1.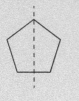

A   B   C   D

2.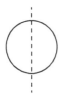

A   B   C   D

3.

A   B   C   D

4.

A   B   C   D

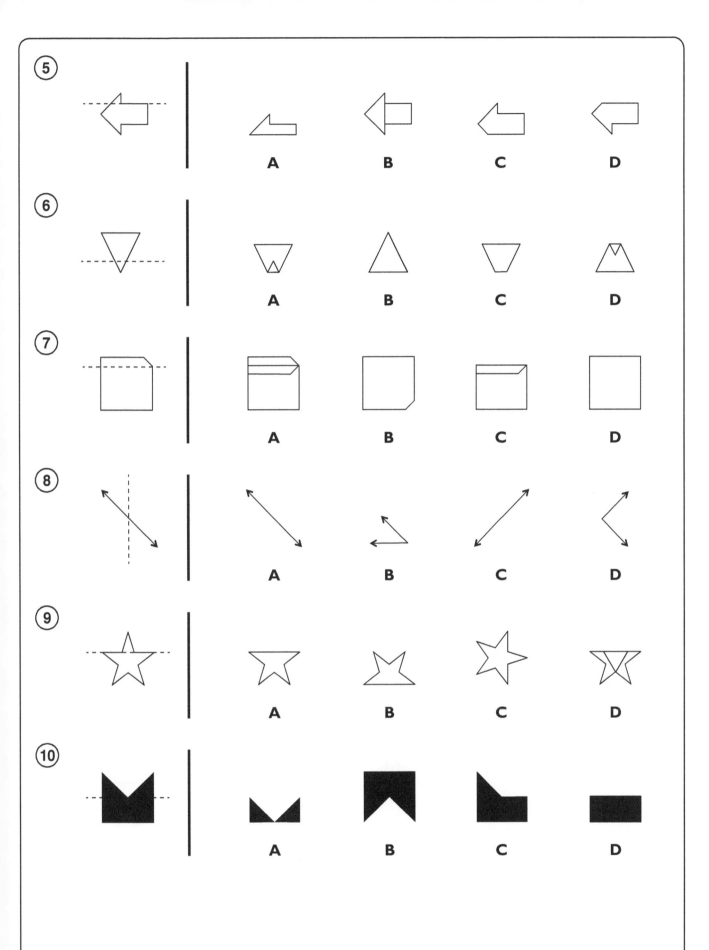

⑤   A   B   C   D

⑥   A   B   C   D

⑦   A   B   C   D

⑧   A   B   C   D

⑨   A   B   C   D

⑩   A   B   C   D

Score: .... / 10

Test 5

You have 5 minutes to complete this test.

You have 10 questions to complete within the given time.

In each question, the first row of figures shows how a square is folded and then holes are punched into it.

Circle the letter below the figure that correctly shows the unfolded square.

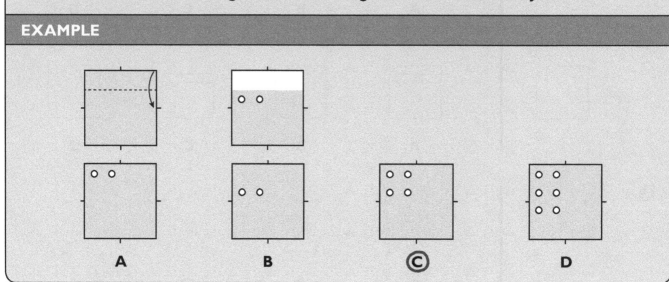

A   B   ©   D

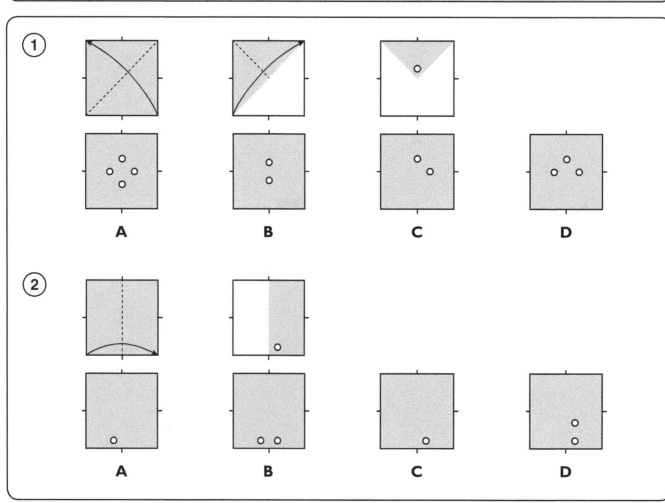

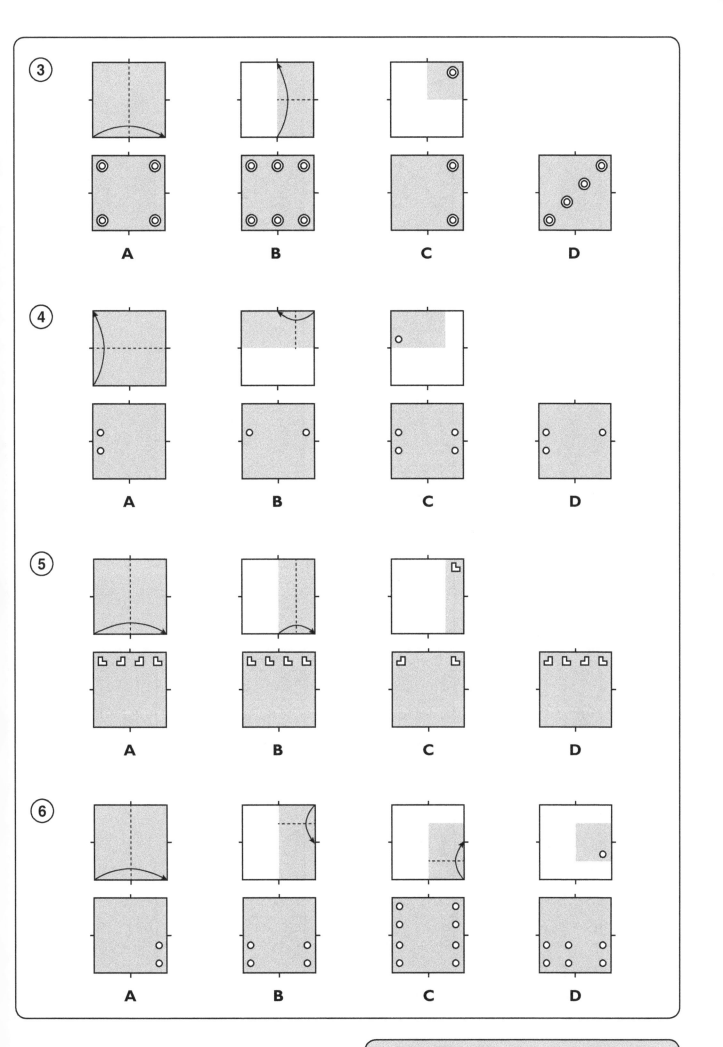

Questions continue on next page

15

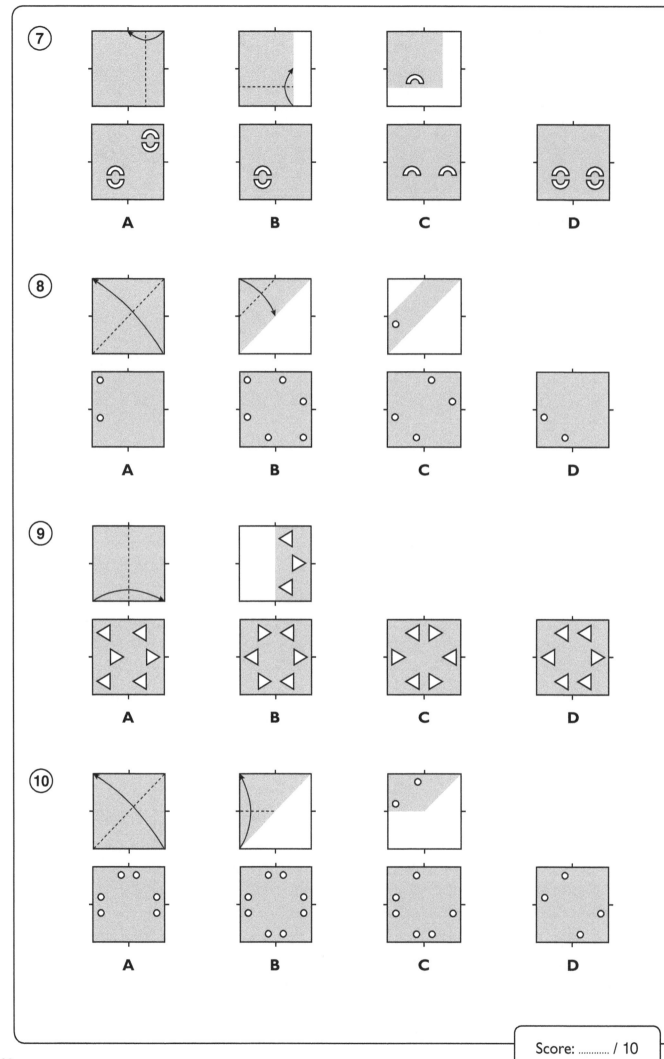

Score: .... / 10

Test 6

You have 5 minutes to complete this test.

You have 10 questions to complete within the given time.

In each question, circle the letter below the figure on the right that shows the <u>top-down 2D view</u> of the 3D figure on the left.

EXAMPLE

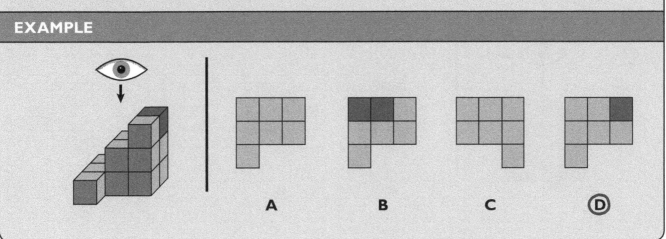

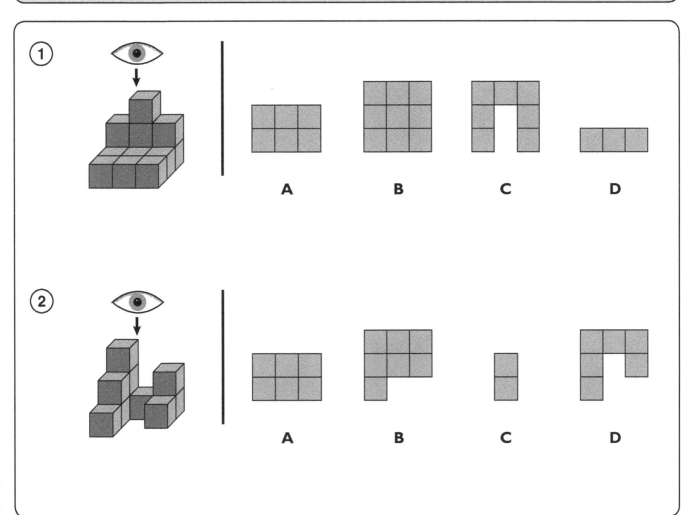

Questions continue on next page

17

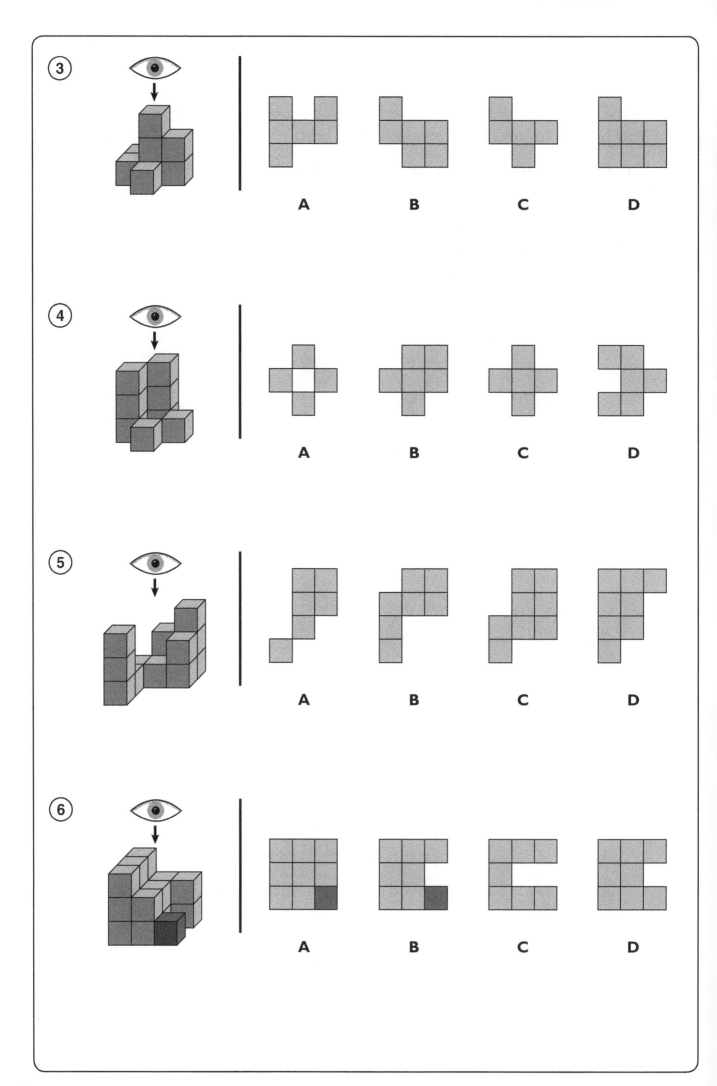

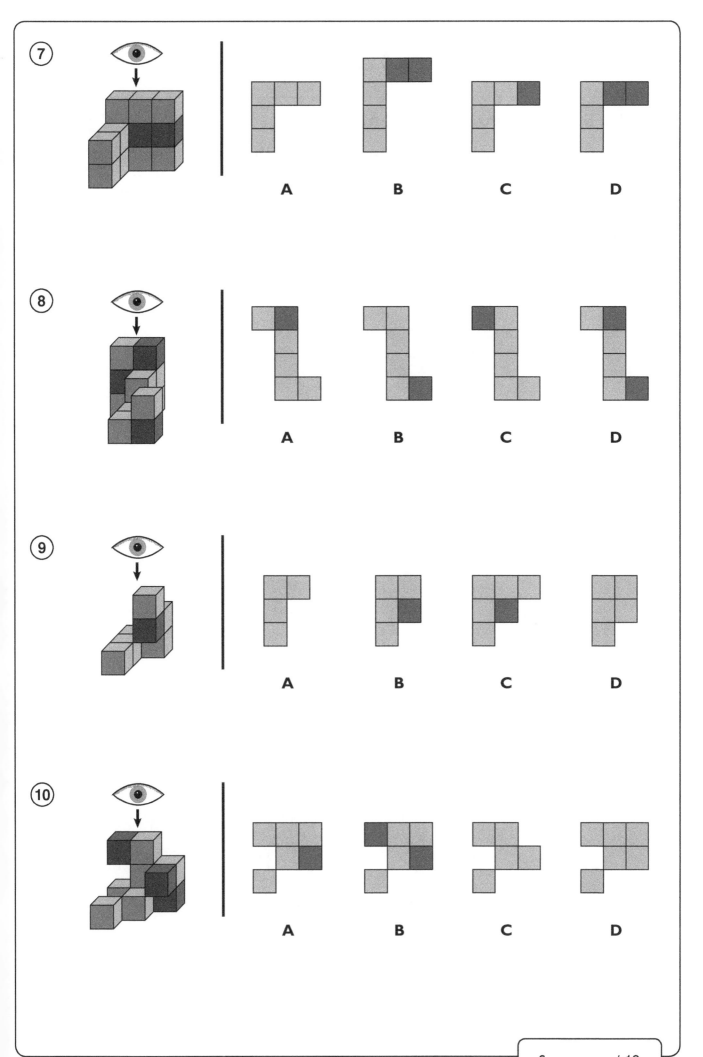

Test 7

You have 5 minutes to complete this test.

You have 10 questions to complete within the given time.

In each question, circle the letter below the figure that shows how the 3D figure on the left could look when viewed looking <u>down from above</u>.

EXAMPLE

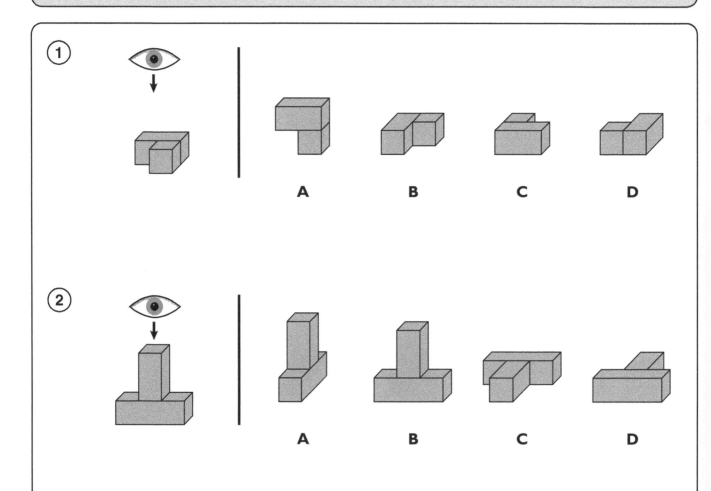

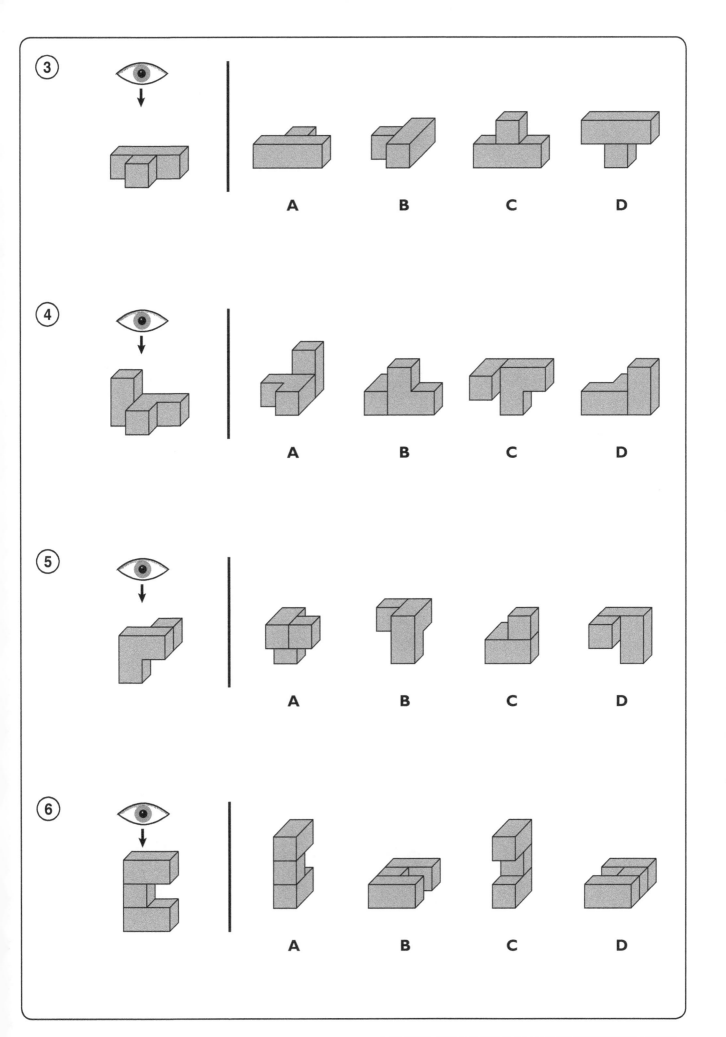

Questions continue on next page

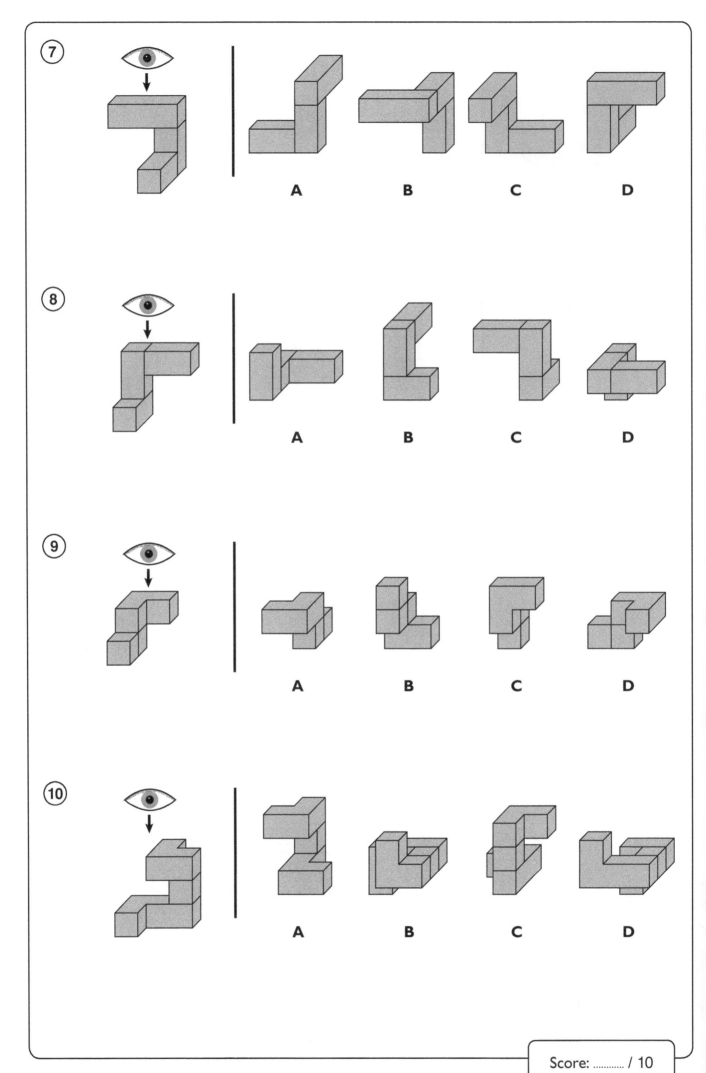

Score: .... / 10

Test 8

You have 6 minutes to complete this test.

You have 10 questions to complete within the given time.

In each question, circle the letter below the cube that can be formed when folding the net on the left.

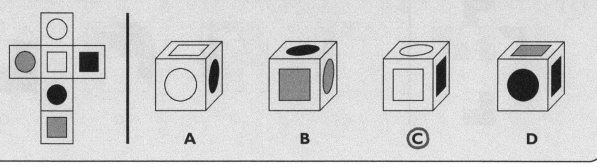

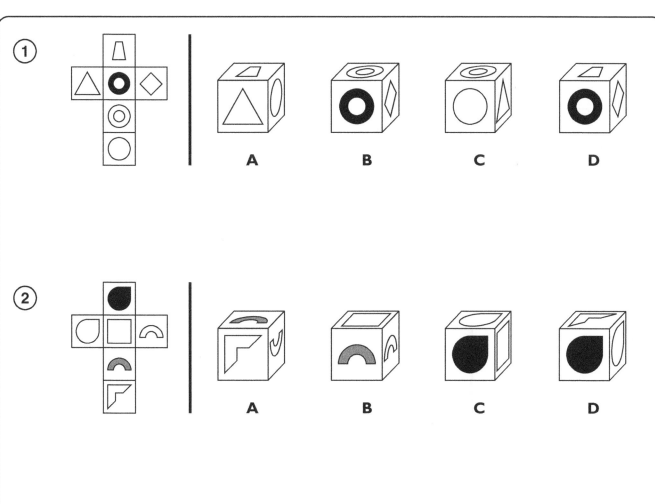

Questions continue on next page

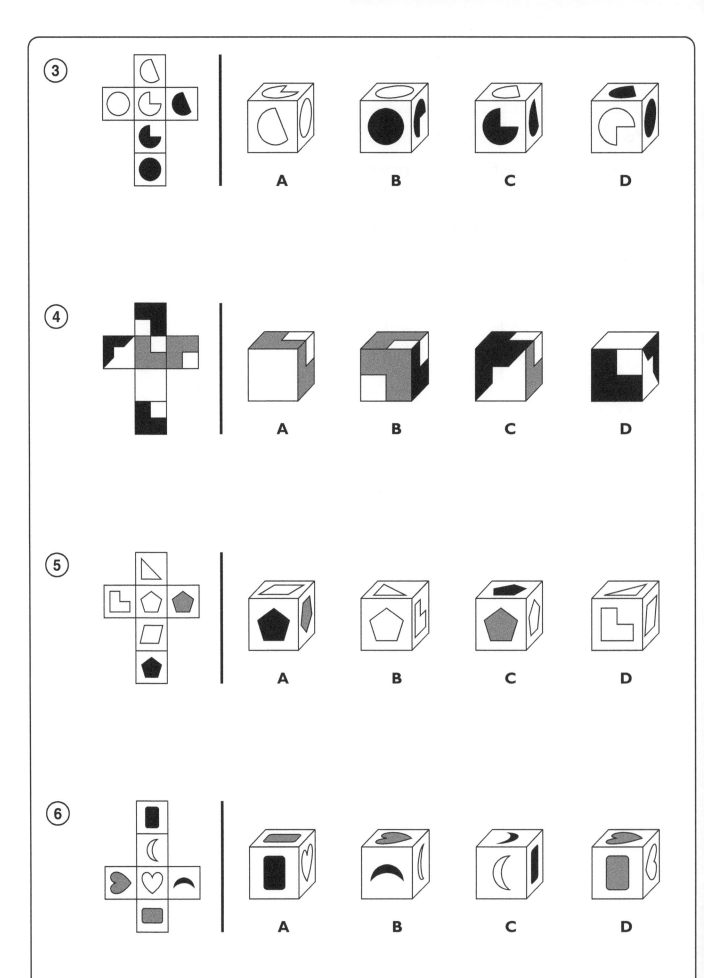

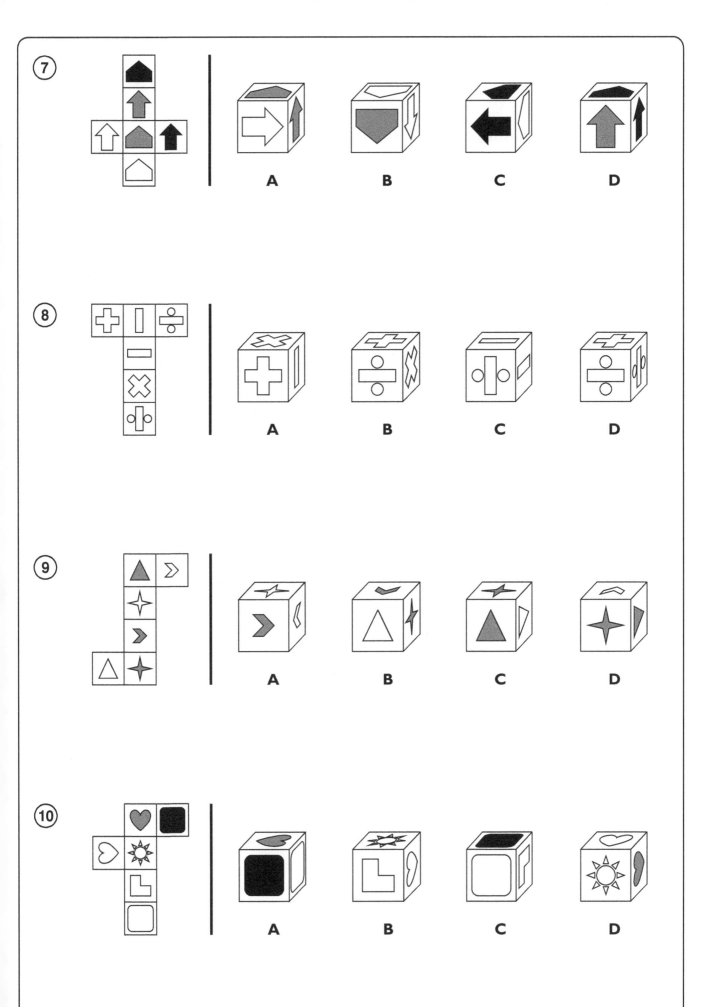

Test 9

You have 5 minutes to complete this test.

You have 8 questions to complete within the given time.

In each question, circle the letter below the net that can be folded to make the cube on the left.

EXAMPLE

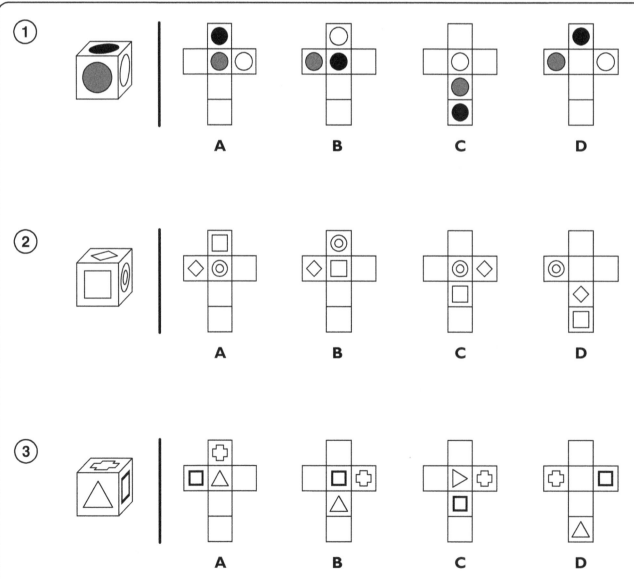

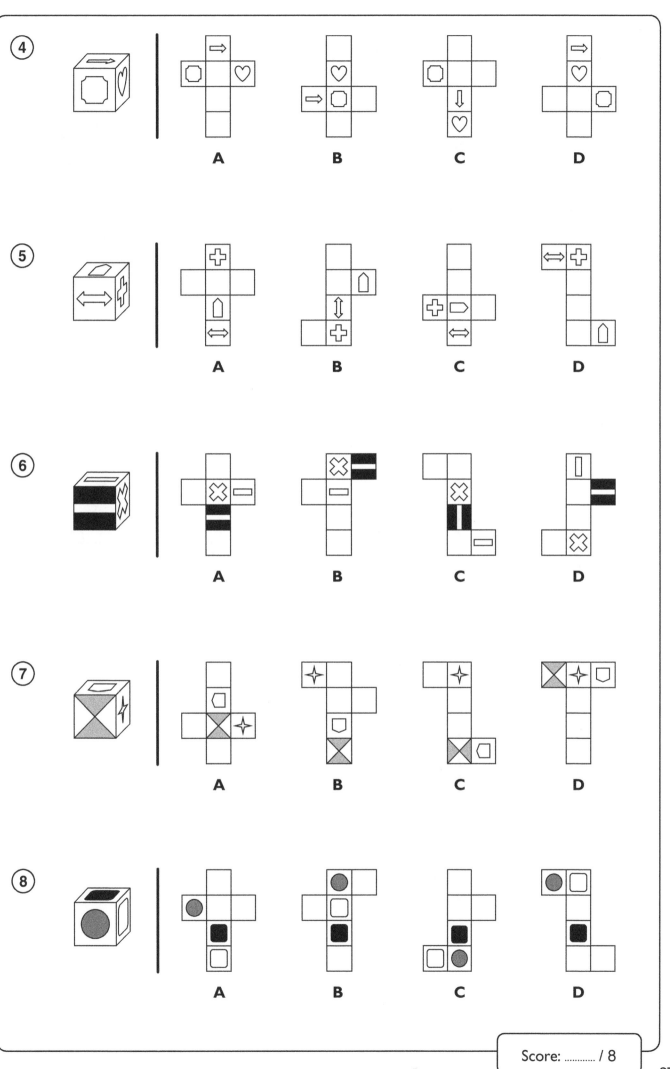

Score: .... / 8

27

Test 10

You have 5 minutes to complete this test.

You have 10 questions to complete within the given time.

In each question, circle the letter below the 3D shape that can be formed from the net on the left.

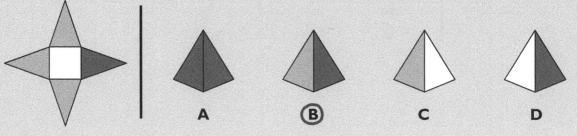

A   (B)   C   D

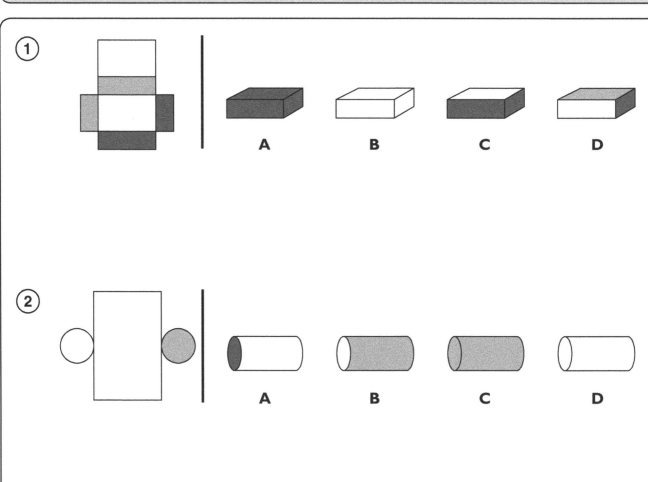

① A   B   C   D

② A   B   C   D

28

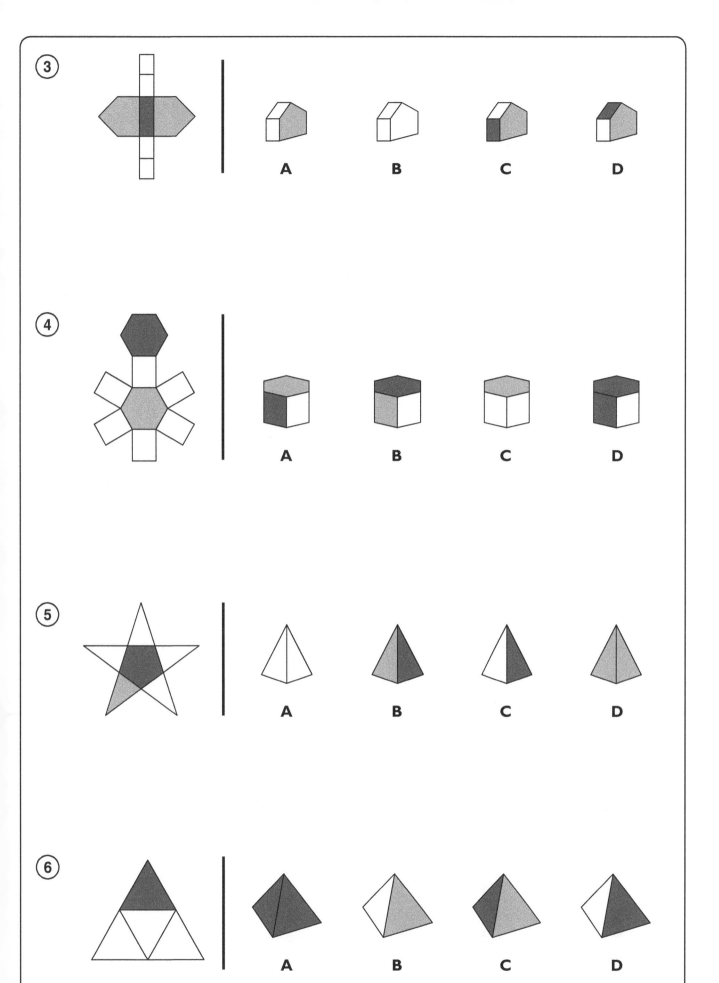

Questions continue on next page

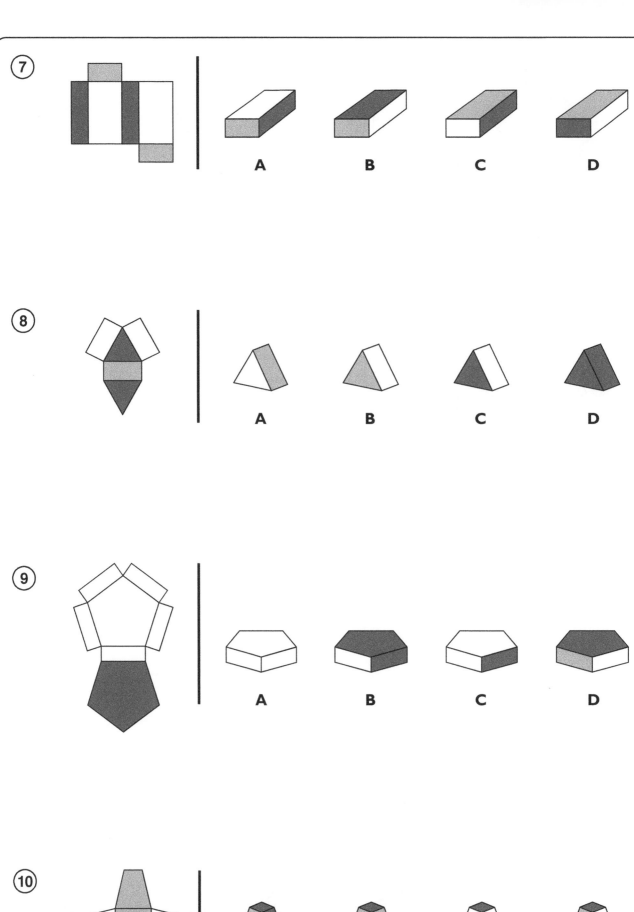

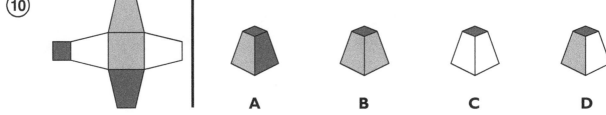

Score: .... / 10

Test 11

You have 5 minutes to complete this test.

You have 10 questions to complete within the given time.

In each question, the figures on the left show different views of the same cube.

Every face of this cube is different.

Circle the letter below the figure that should replace the blank face.

EXAMPLE

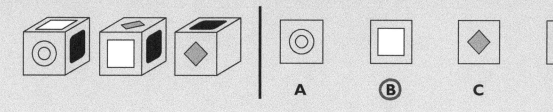

A   B   C   D

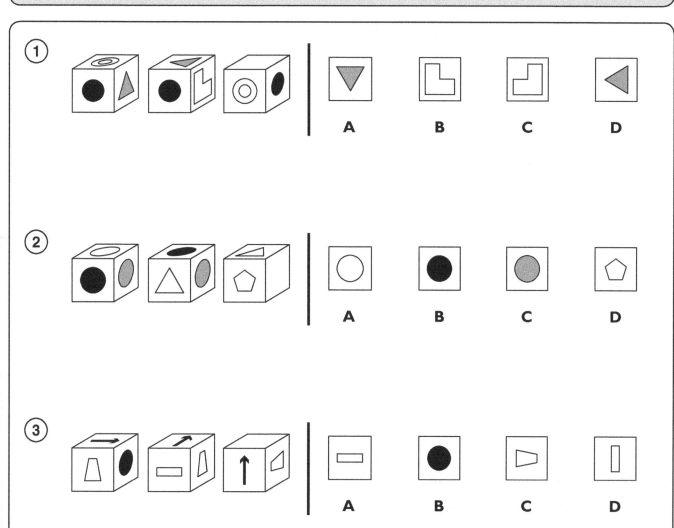

Questions continue on next page

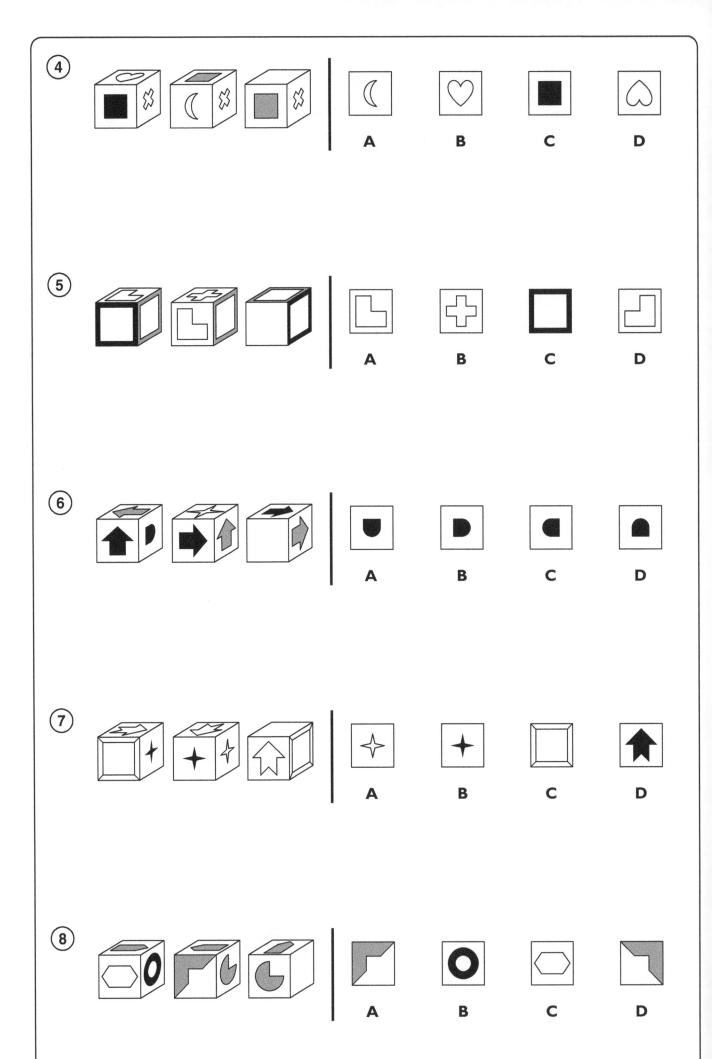

9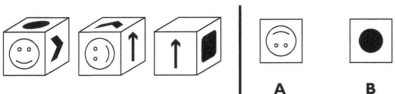

A	**B**	**C**	**D**

10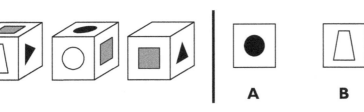

A	**B**	**C**	**D**

Score: .... / 10

Test 12

You have 5 minutes to complete this test.

You have 10 questions to complete within the given time.

In each question, the shape on the left is hidden in one of the figures on the right.

This shape stays exactly the same size and does not get rotated or flipped over.

Circle the letter below the figure that contains the hidden shape.

EXAMPLE

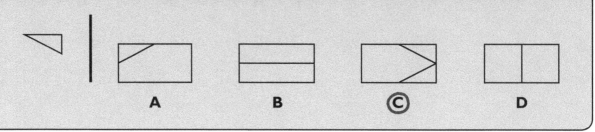

| A | B | Ⓒ | D |

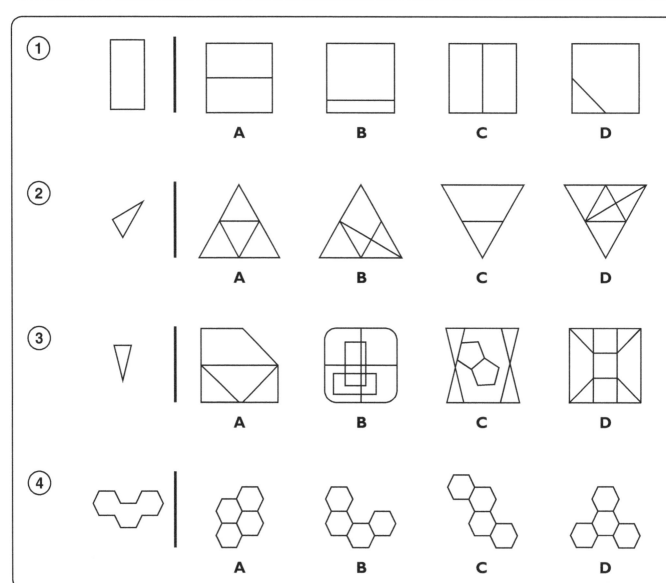

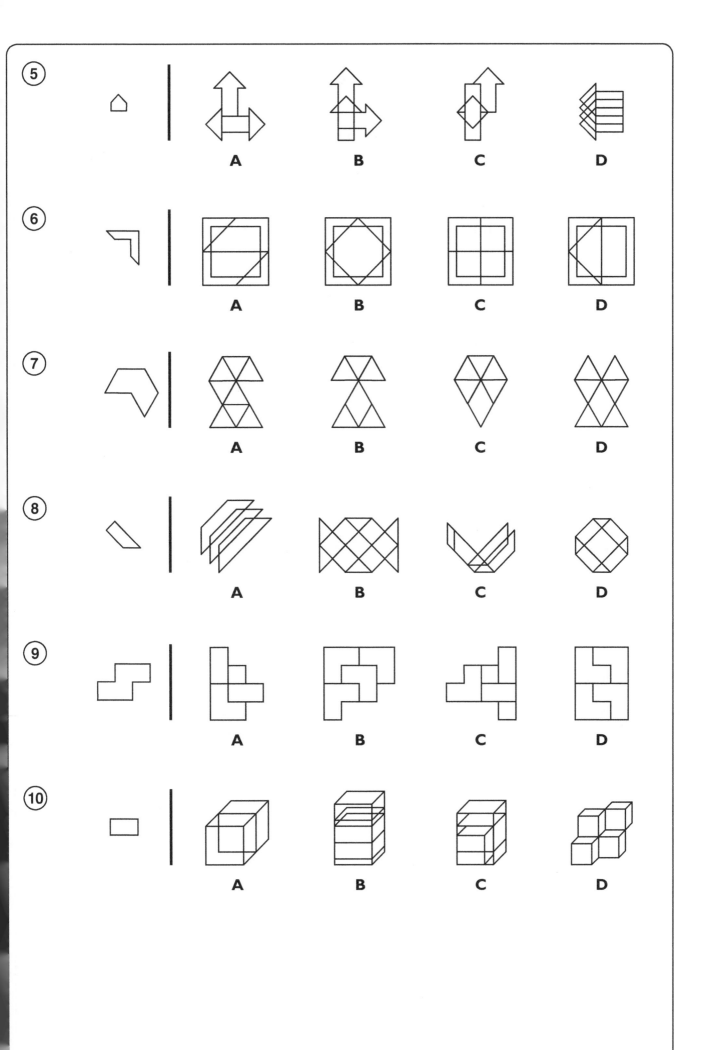

⑤

A　B　C　D

⑥

A　B　C　D

⑦

A　B　C　D

⑧

A　B　C　D

⑨

A　B　C　D

⑩

A　B　C　D

Score: .... / 10

35

Test 13

You have 6 minutes to complete this test.

You have 12 questions to complete within the given time.

In each question, circle the letter below the set of blocks that can be combined to make the figure on the left.

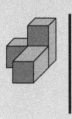

A

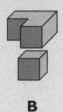

B

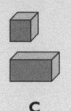

C

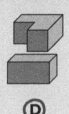

Ⓓ

①

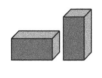

A

B

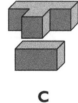

C

D

②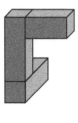

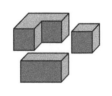

A

B

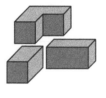

C

D

③

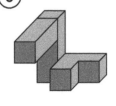

A

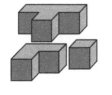

B

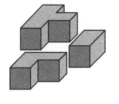

C

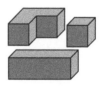

D

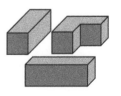

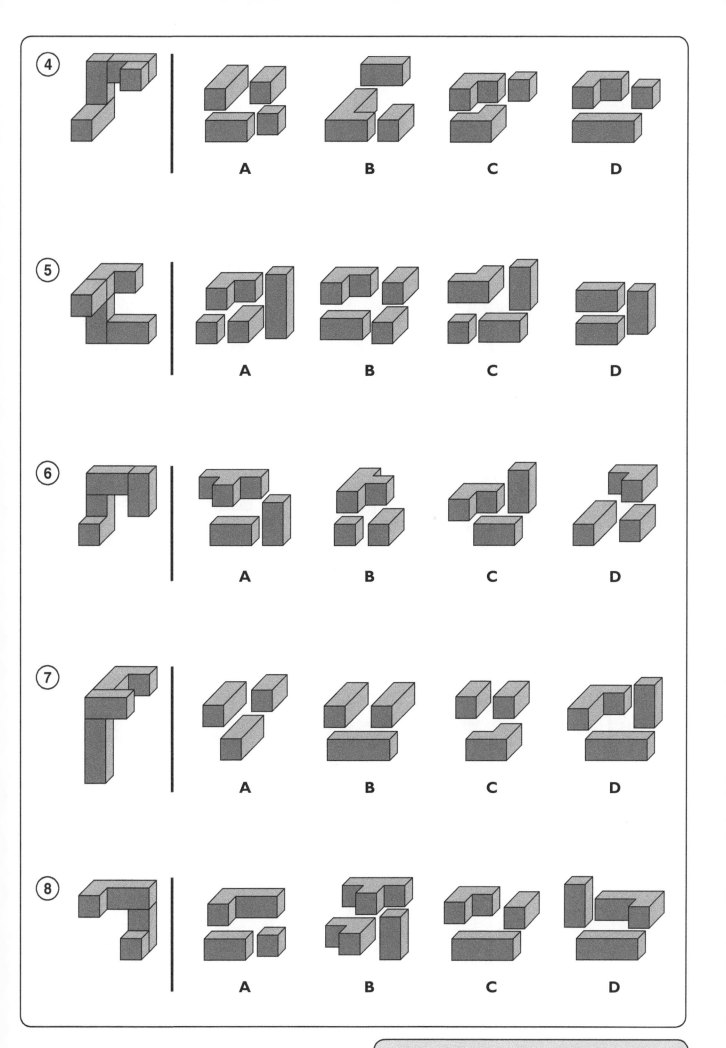

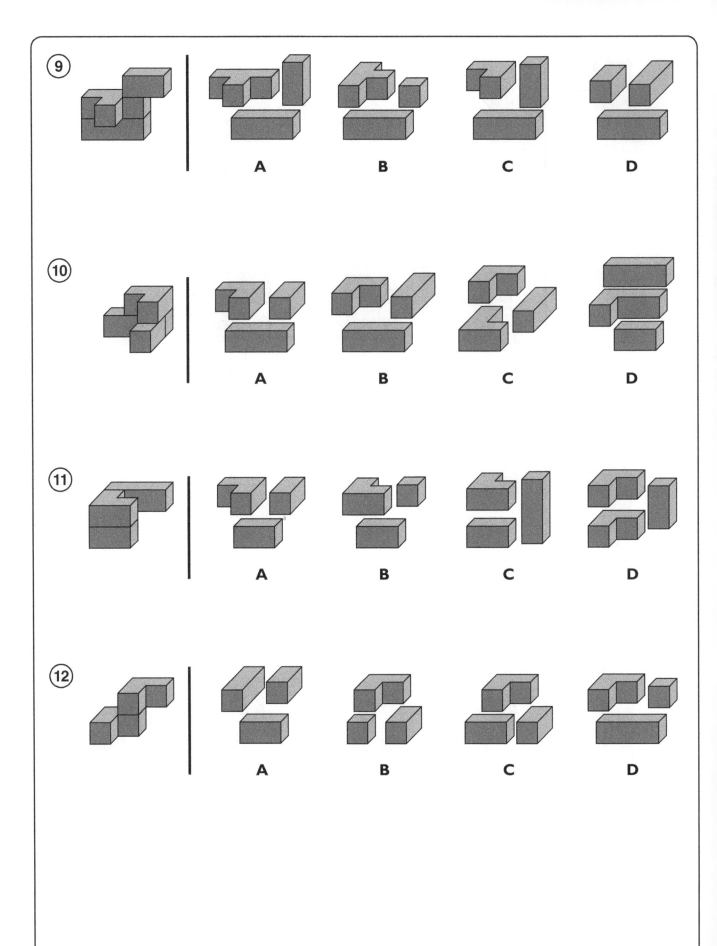

Score: .... / 12

Test 14

You have 5 minutes to complete this test.

You have 10 questions to complete within the given time.

In each question, circle the letter below the figure that can be combined with the first figure to create the shape in the grey box. The first figure must not be rotated.

EXAMPLE

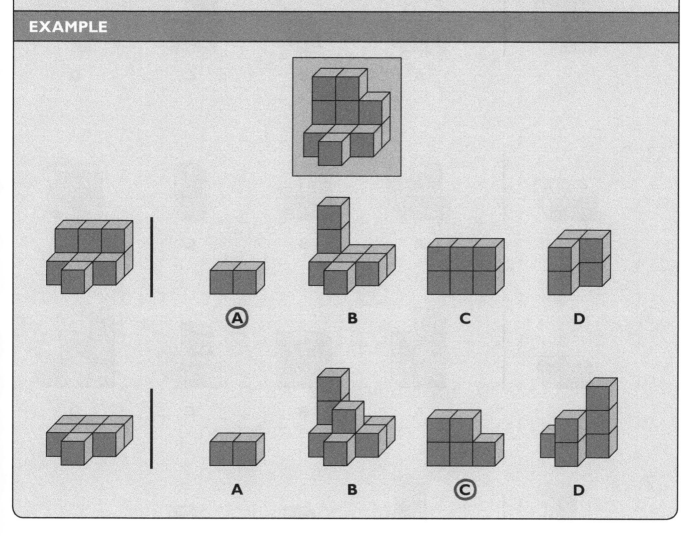

Questions start on next page

Refer to the shape in the grey box for Questions 1–5 below.

① 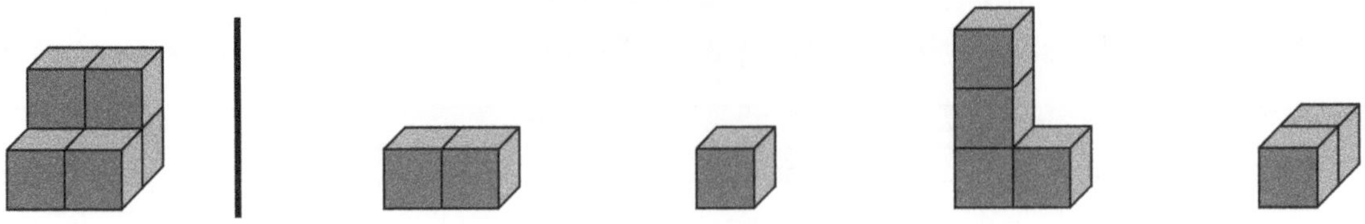   A   B   C   D

②   A   B   C   D

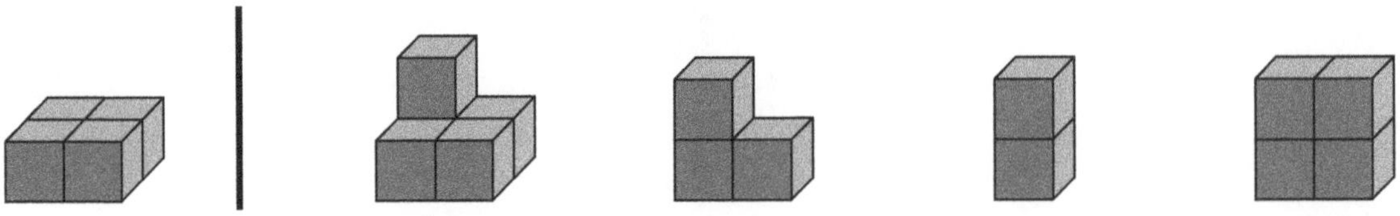

③   A   B   C   D

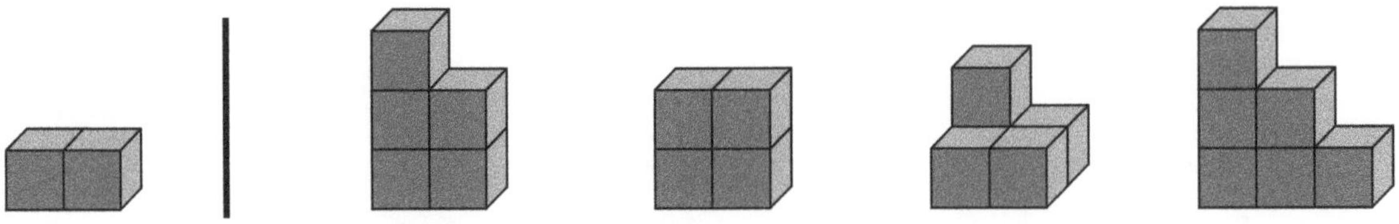

④   A   B   C   D

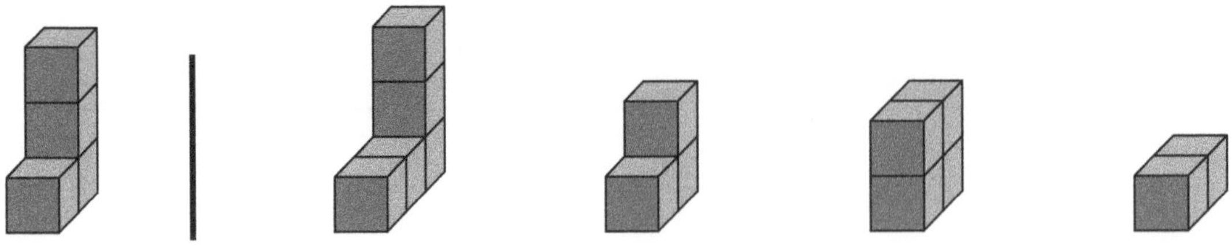

⑤   A   B   C   D

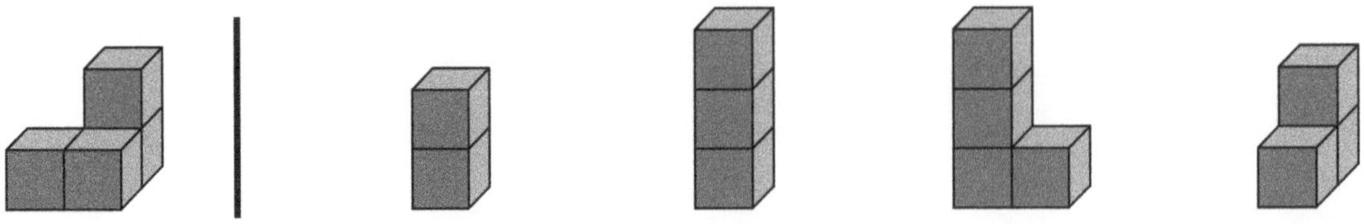

Refer to the shape in the grey box for Questions 6–10 below.

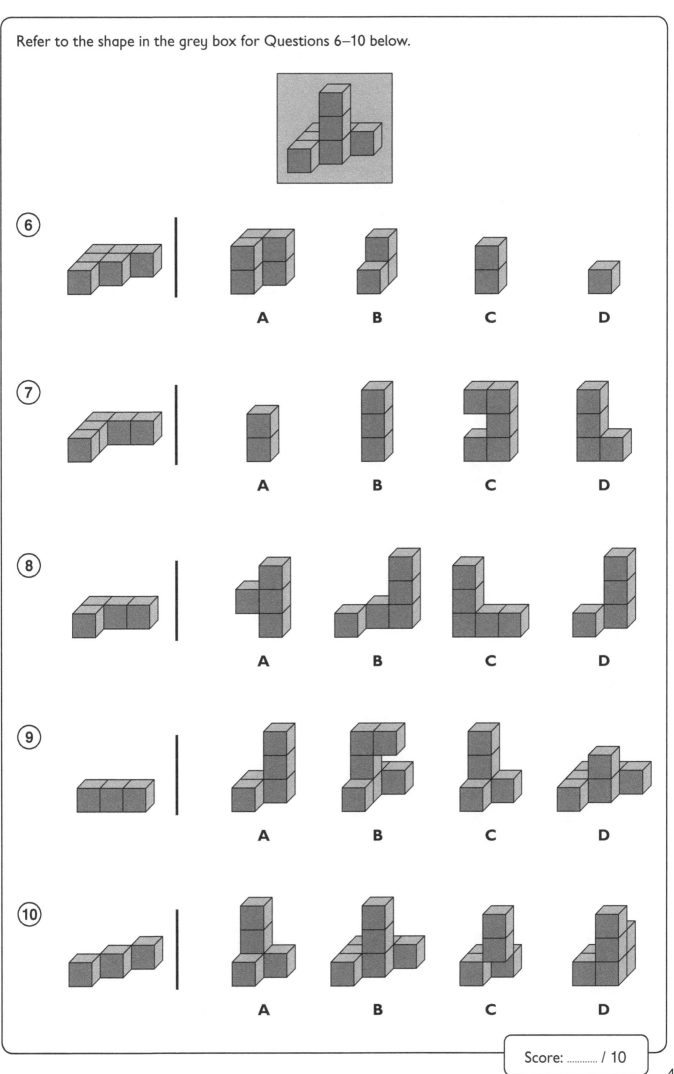

6

A   B   C   D

7

A   B   C   D

8

A   B   C   D

9

A   B   C   D

10

A   B   C   D

Score: .... / 10

Test 15

You have 6 minutes to complete this test.

You have 12 questions to complete within the given time.

In each question, one of the 3D figures below has been rotated to create the figure shown. Circle the letter of the figure that has been rotated.

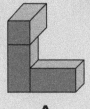

A

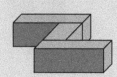

D

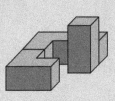

B

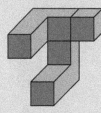

E

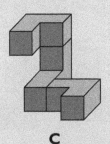

C

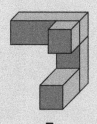

F

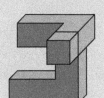

A   D

B   Ⓔ

C   F

①

A   D

B   E

C   F

②

A   D

B   E

C   F

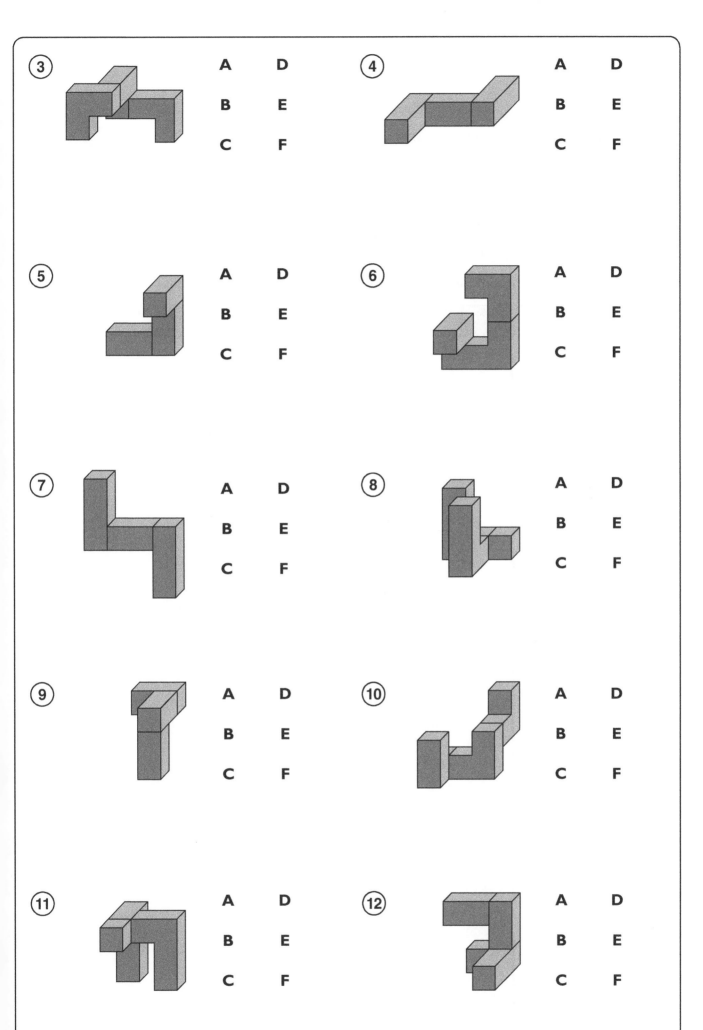

③   A   D   ④   A   D

     B   E   B   E

     C   F   C   F

⑤   A   D   ⑥   A   D

     B   E   B   E

     C   F   C   F

⑦   A   D   ⑧   A   D

     B   E   B   E

     C   F   C   F

⑨   A   D   ⑩   A   D

     B   E   B   E

     C   F   C   F

⑪   A   D   ⑫   A   D

     B   E   B   E

     C   F   C   F

Score: .... / 12

Test 16

You have 5 minutes to complete this test.

You have 10 questions to complete within the given time.

In each question, circle the letter below the figure that shows how the left-hand figure will look when folded along the dotted line.

The fold should be made towards the dotted line, not away from it.

EXAMPLE

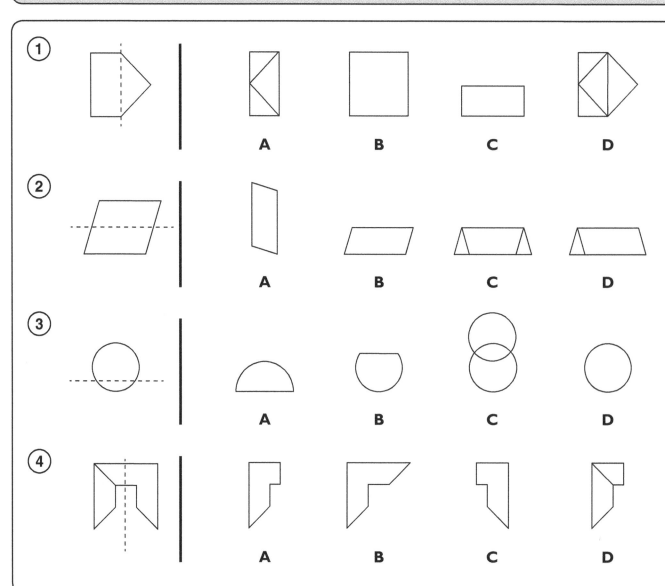

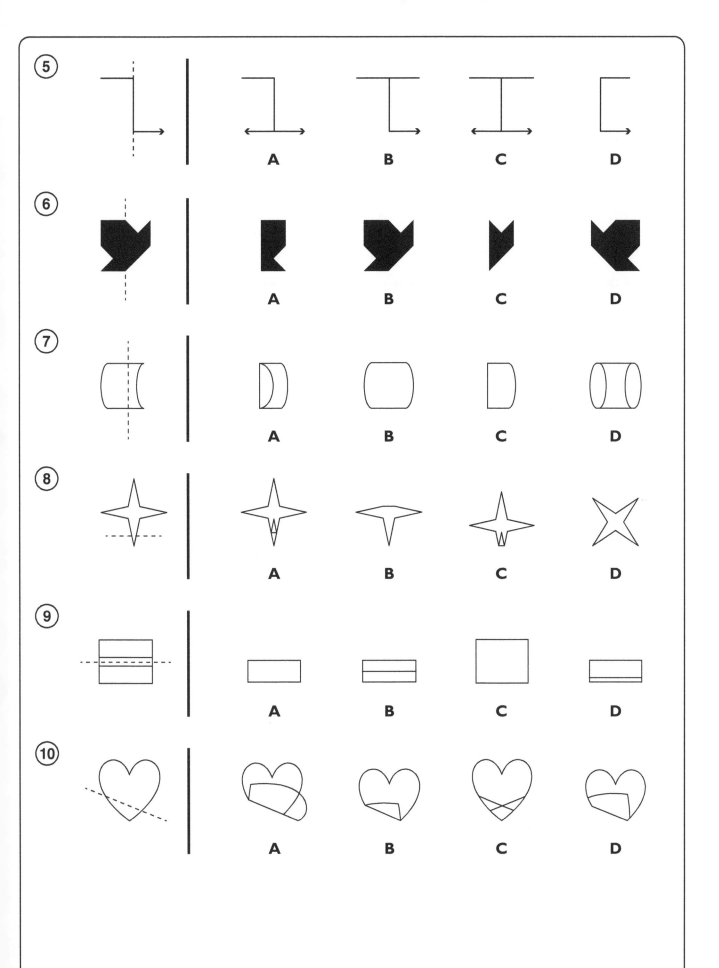

Test 17

You have 5 minutes to complete this test.

You have 10 questions to complete within the given time.

In each question, the first row of figures shows how a square is folded and then holes are punched into it.

Circle the letter below the figure that correctly shows the unfolded square.

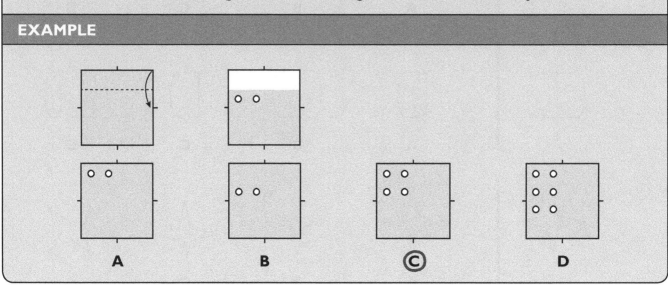

A   B   C   D

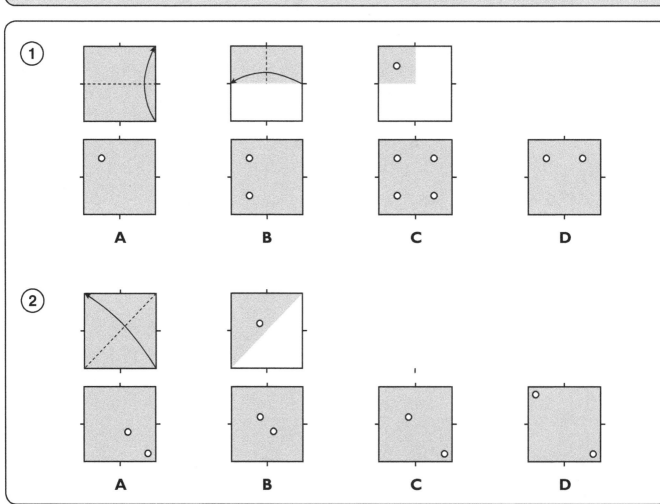

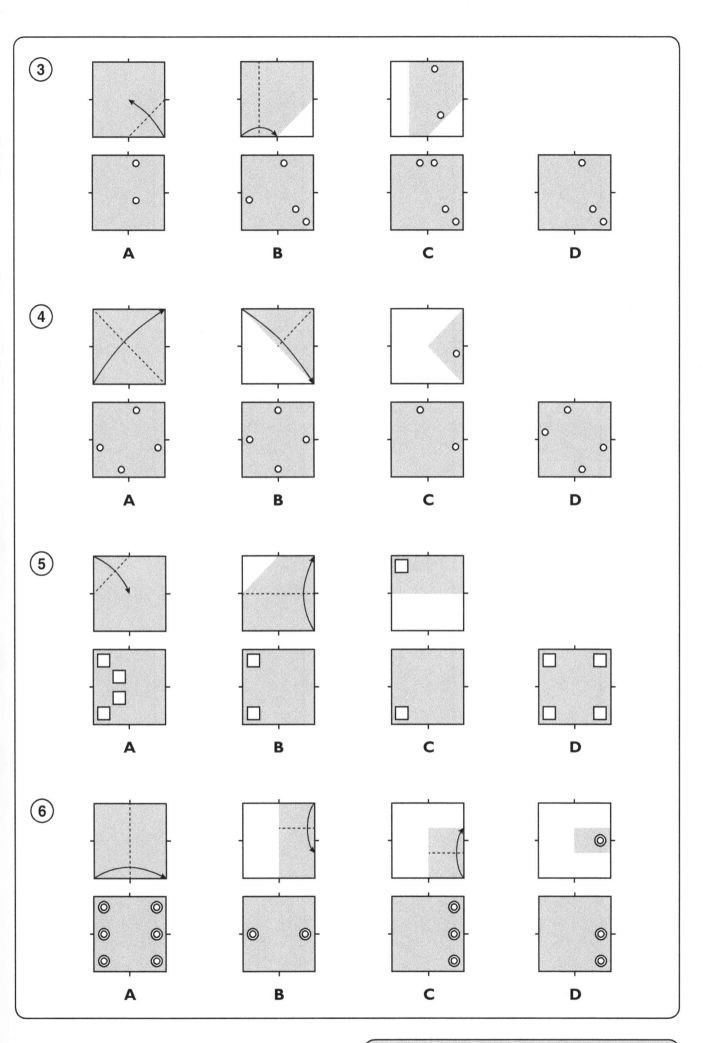

Questions continue on next page

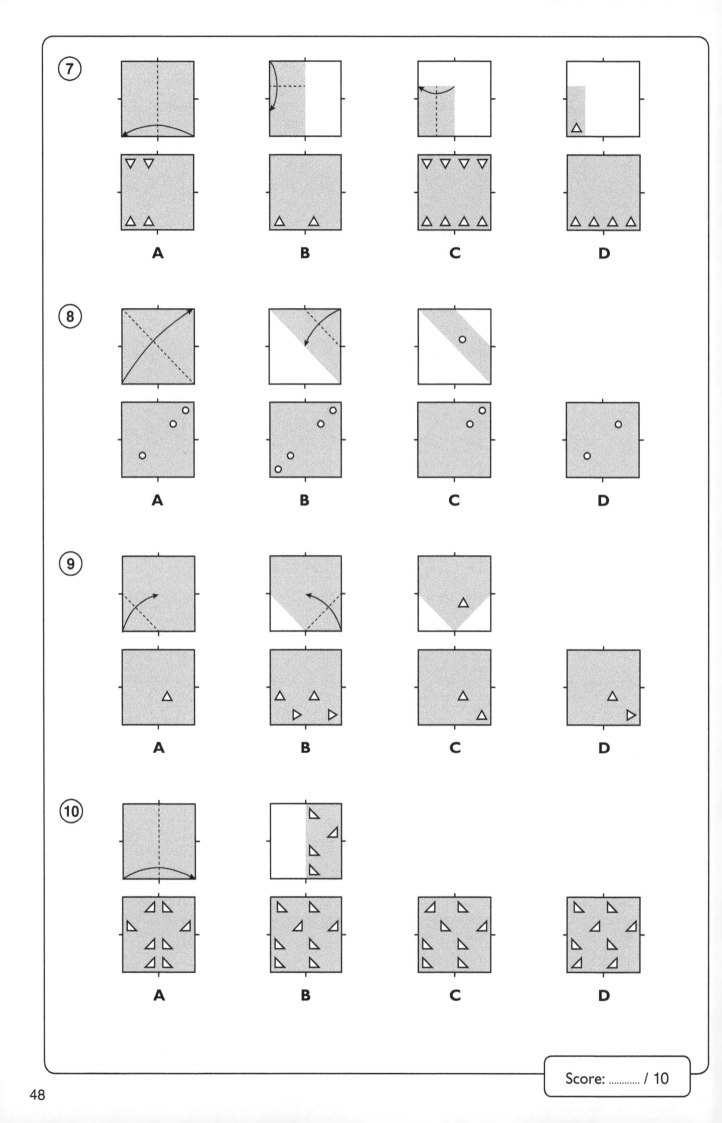

Score: .... / 10

Test 18

You have 5 minutes to complete this test.

You have 10 questions to complete within the given time.

In each question, circle the letter below the figure on the right that shows the 2D side view of the 3D figure on the left, when viewed from the <u>right</u>.

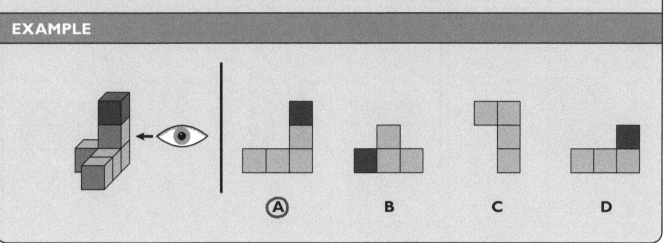

①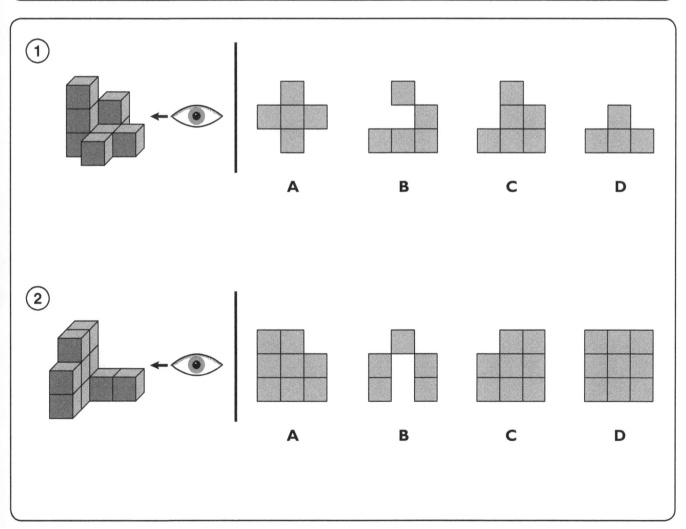

②

Questions continue on next page

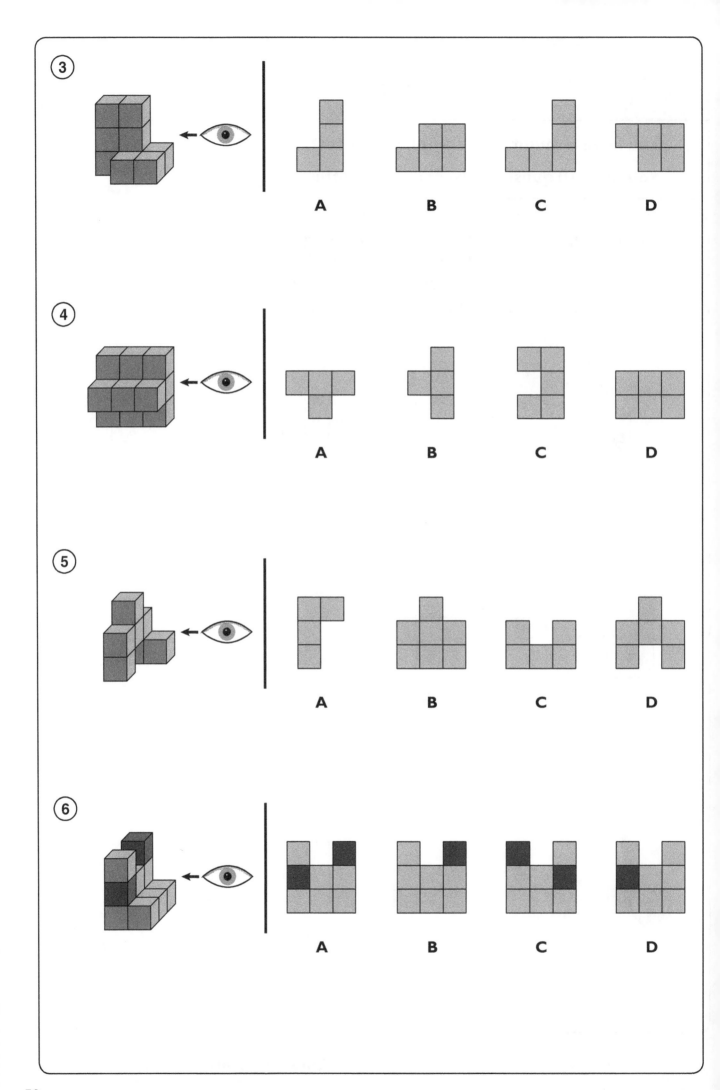

3

A   B   C   D

4

A   B   C   D

5

A   B   C   D

6

A   B   C   D

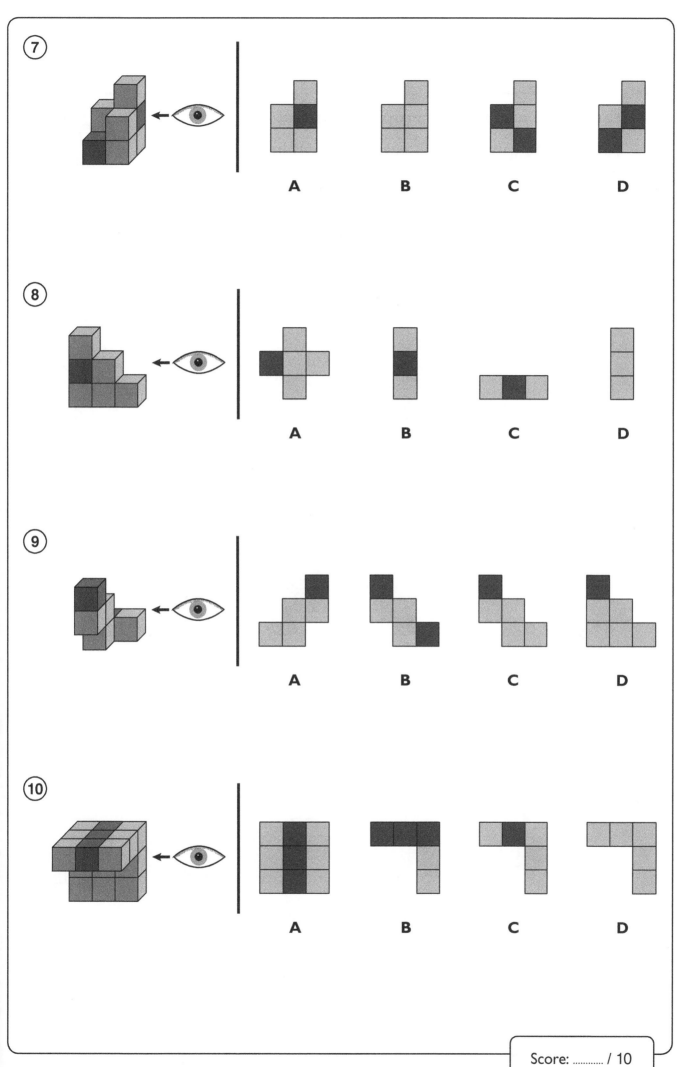

Test 19

You have 5 minutes to complete this test.

You have 10 questions to complete within the given time.

In each question, circle the letter below the figure that shows how the 3D figure on the left could look when viewed from <u>behind</u>.

EXAMPLE

A   B   ©   D

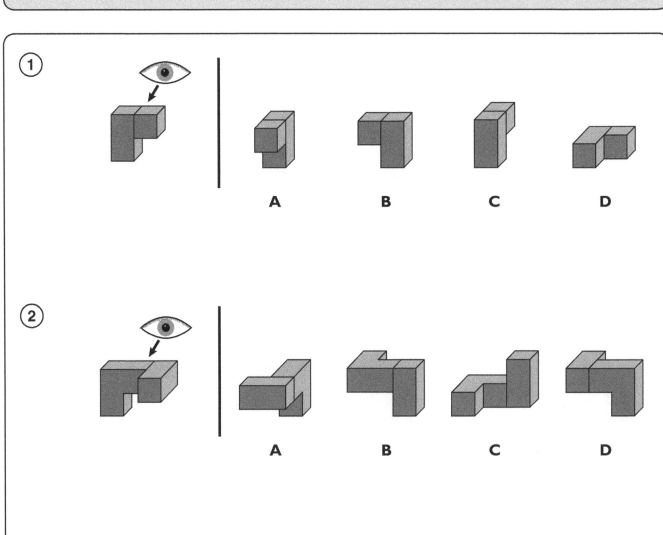

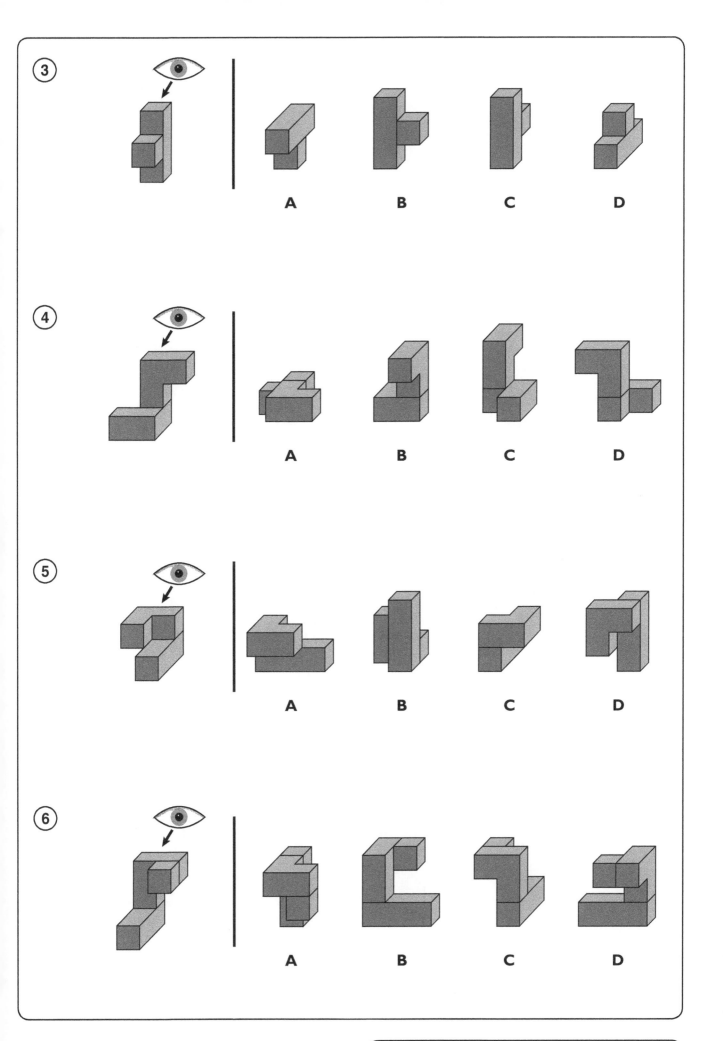

Questions continue on next page

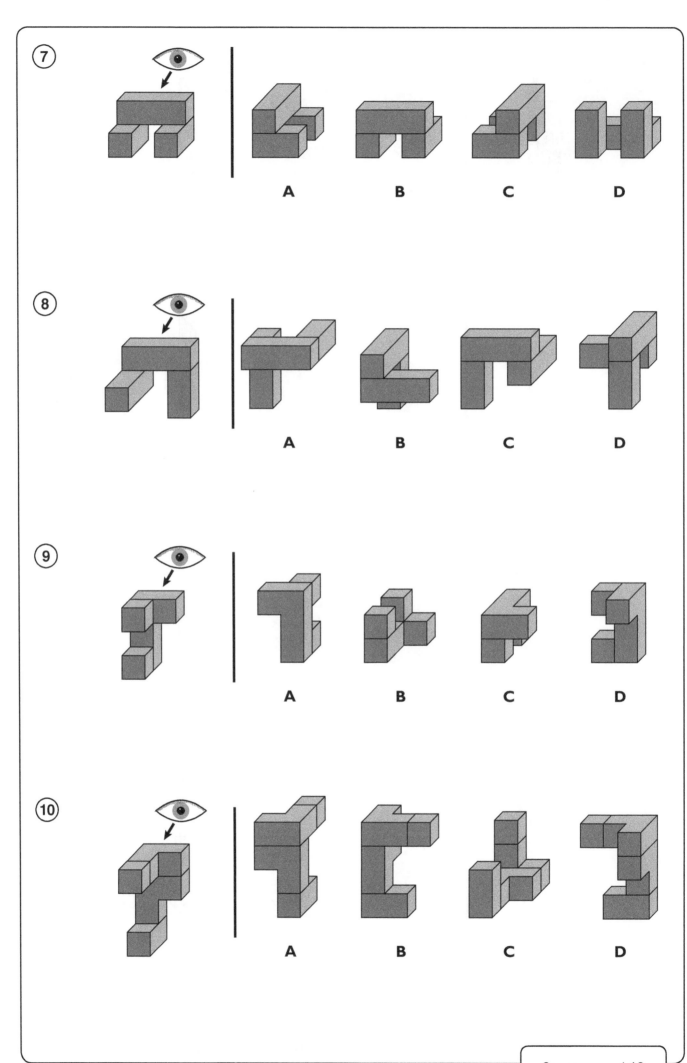

Score: .... / 10

Test 20

You have 6 minutes to complete this test.

You have 10 questions to complete within the given time.

In each question, circle the letter below the cube that can be formed when folding the net on the left.

EXAMPLE

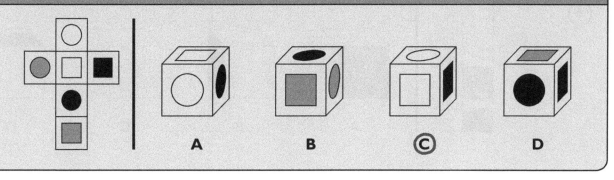

A   B   ©   D

①

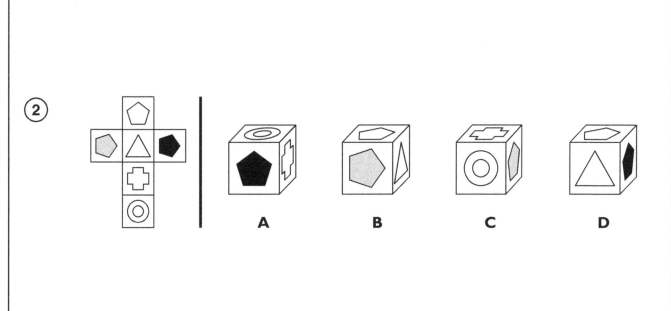

A   B   C   D

②

A   B   C   D

Questions continue on next page

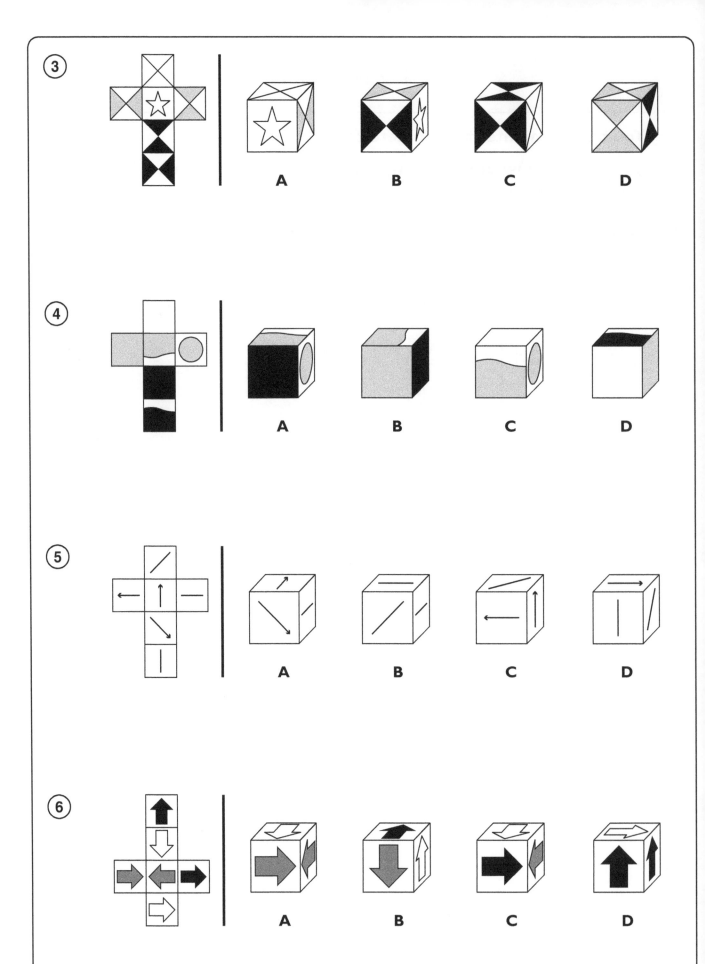

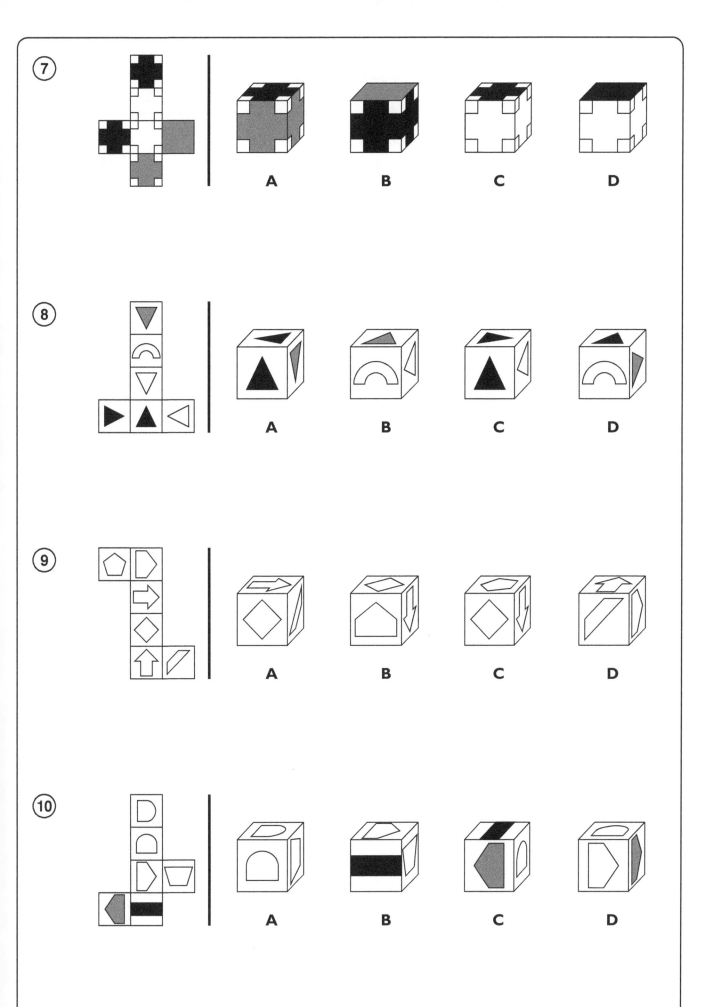

Test 21

You have 5 minutes to complete this test.

You have 8 questions to complete within the given time.

In each question, circle the letter below the net that can be folded to make the cube on the left.

EXAMPLE

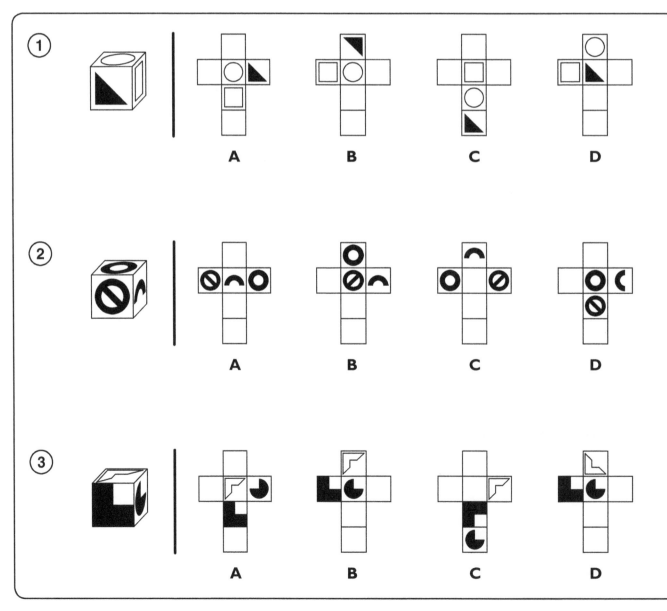

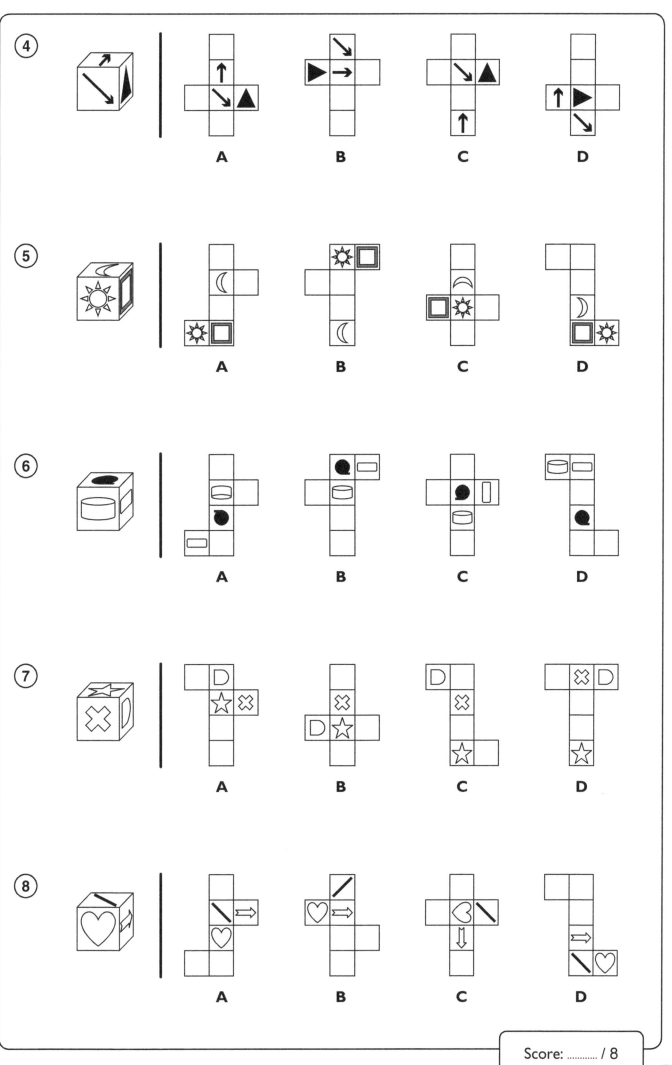

59

Test 22

You have 5 minutes to complete this test.

You have 10 questions to complete within the given time.

In each question, circle the letter below the 3D shape that can be formed from the net on the left.

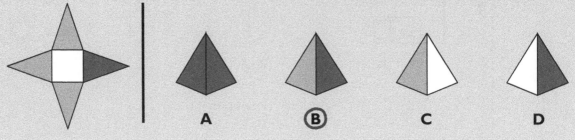

①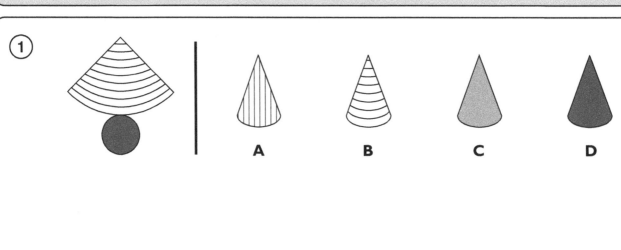

②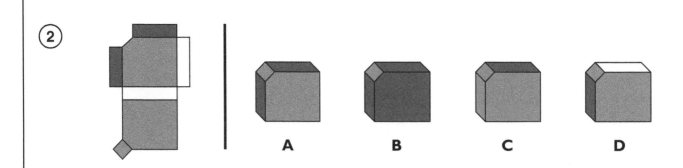

60

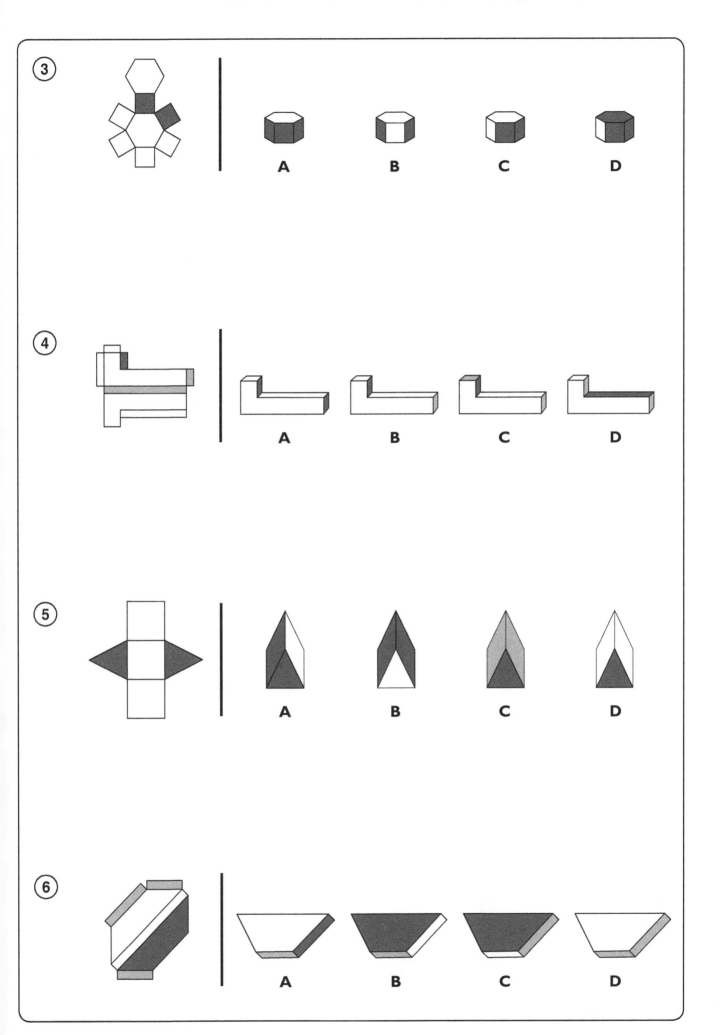

Questions continue on next page

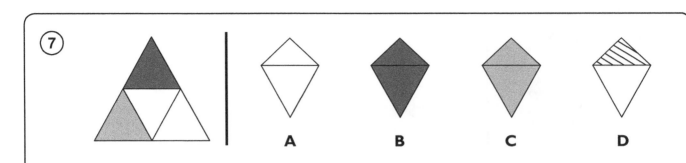

⑦   A   B   C   D

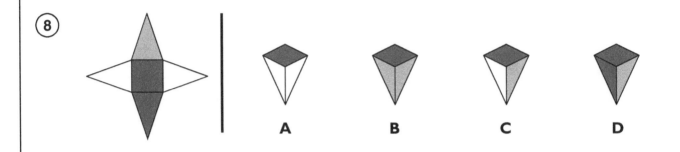

⑧   A   B   C   D

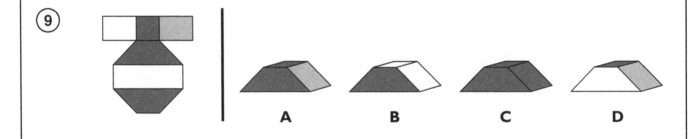

⑨   A   B   C   D

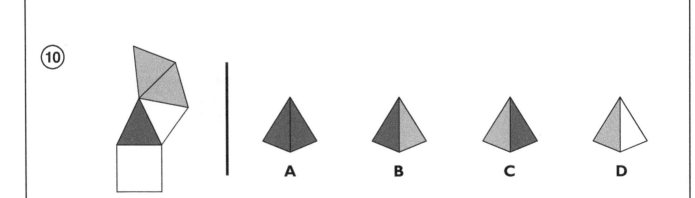

⑩   A   B   C   D

Score: .... / 10

Test 23

You have 5 minutes to complete this test.

You have 10 questions to complete within the given time.

In each question, the figures on the left show different views of the same cube.

Every face of this cube is different.

Circle the letter below the figure that should replace the blank face.

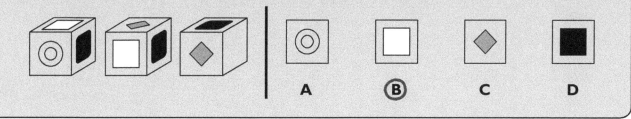

A   (B)   C   D

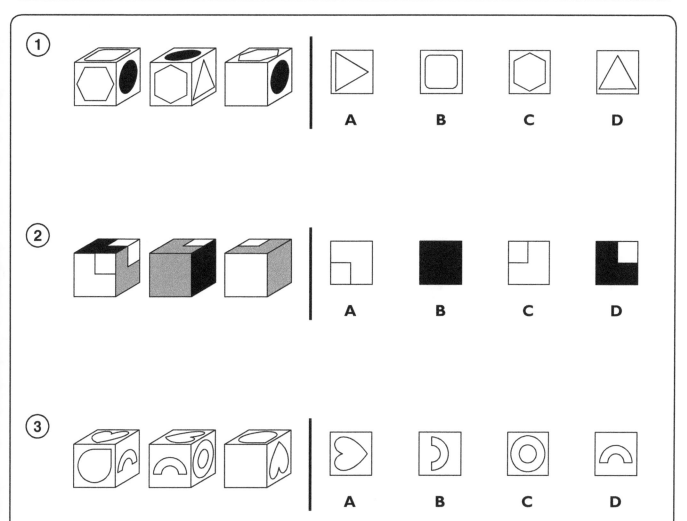

①   A   B   C   D

②   A   B   C   D

③   A   B   C   D

Questions continue on next page

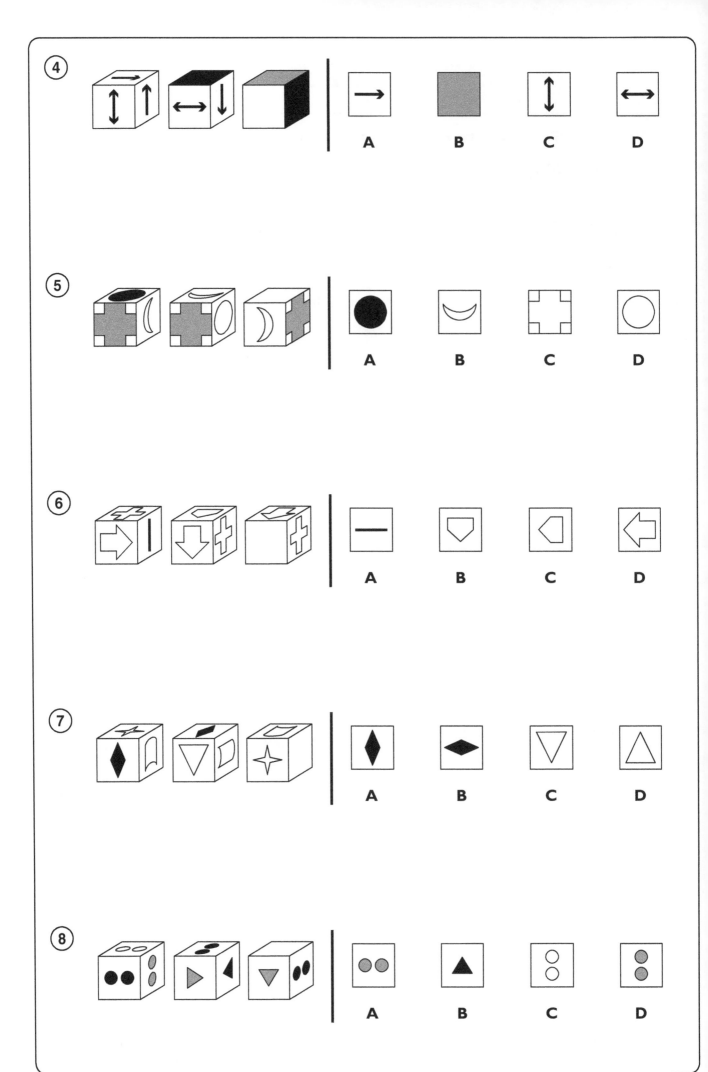

4   A   B   C   D

5   A   B   C   D

6   A   B   C   D

7   A   B   C   D

8   A   B   C   D

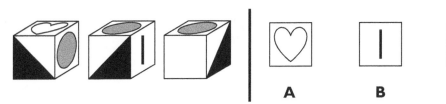

A B C D

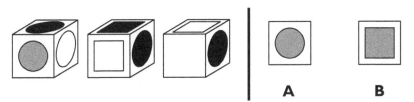

10

A B C D

Score: .... / 10

Test 24

You have 5 minutes to complete this test.

You have 10 questions to complete within the given time.

In each question, the shape on the left is hidden in one of the figures on the right.

This shape stays exactly the same size and does not get rotated or flipped over.

Circle the letter below the figure that contains the hidden shape.

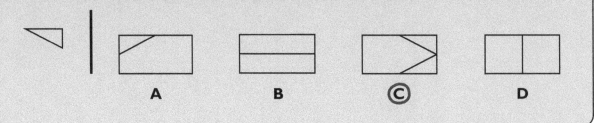

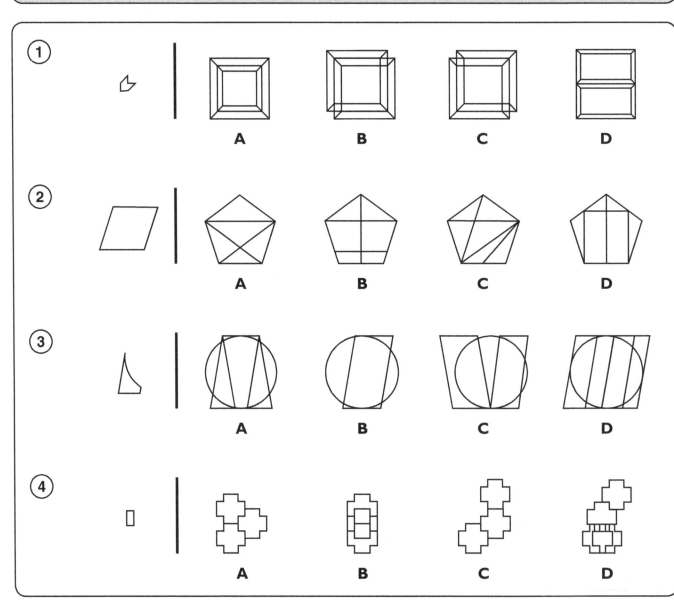

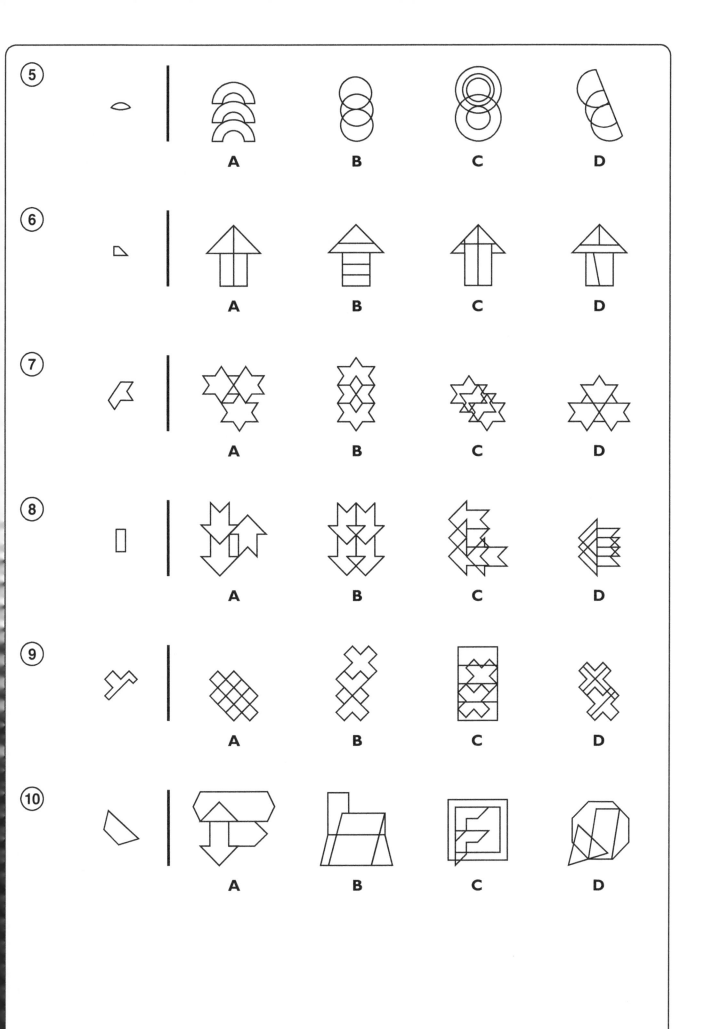

5 A B C D

6 A B C D

7 A B C D

8 A B C D

9 A B C D

10 A B C D

Test 25

You have 5 minutes to complete this test.

You have 10 questions to complete within the given time.

In each question, circle the letter below the figure on the right that shows the <u>2D rear view</u> of the 3D figure on the left.

EXAMPLE

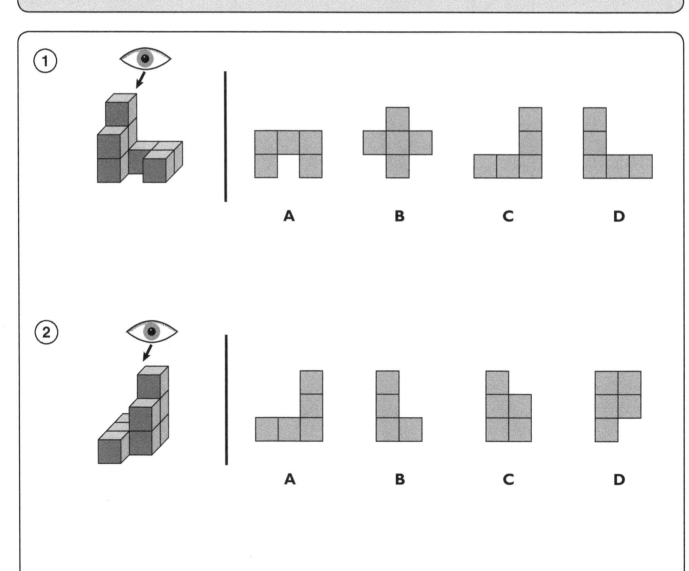

A   (B)   C   D

①

A   B   C   D

②

A   B   C   D

68

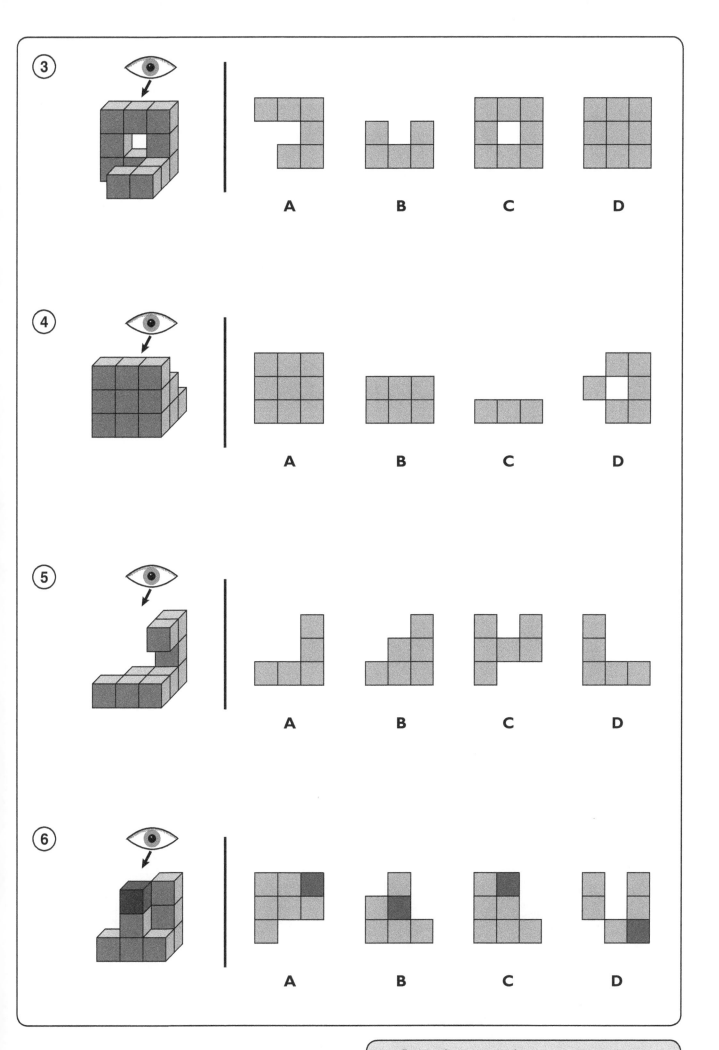

Questions continue on next page

69

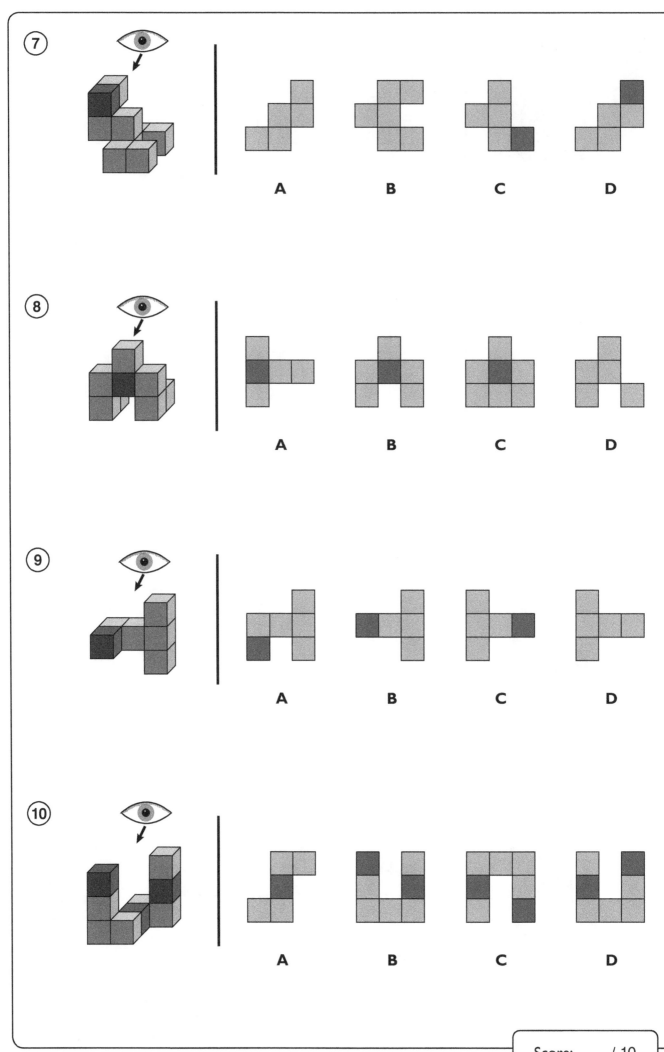

Score: ………… / 10

Answers

Test 1

Q1   A

Q2   C

Q3   D

Q4   A

Q5   B

Q6   C

Q7   D

Q8   A

Q9   B

Q10   C

Q11   B

Q12   A

Test 2

Q1   B

Q2   D

Q3   C

Q4   C

Q5   B

Q6   D

Q7   D

Q8   B

Q9   B

Q10   D

Test 3

Q1   E
A 180° horizontal rotation.

Q2   B
A 180° vertical rotation.

Q3   C
A 180° vertical rotation.

Q4   A
A 90° vertical rotation backwards.

Q5   F
A 90° horizontal rotation clockwise.

Q6   D
A 90° vertical rotation forwards.

Q7   F
A 180° vertical rotation.

Q8   C
A 180° horizontal rotation.

Q9   E
A 90° horizontal rotation clockwise.

Q10   A
A 90° horizontal rotation anticlockwise.

Q11   B
A 90° horizontal rotation anticlockwise.

Q12   D
A 180° horizontal rotation.

Test 4

Q1   C
The right-hand side folds on top of the left-hand side to form a semicircle.

Q2   B
The top right half folds directly on top of the bottom left half.

Q3   A
The right arrow folds directly on top of the left arrow.

Q4   B
The top right half folds directly on top of the bottom left half.

Q5   C
The bottom section folds up over the top section.

Q6   A
The bottom section folds up over the top section.

Q7   C
The top section folds down over the bottom section.

Q8   D
The arrow on the left folds over on to the right.

Q9   B
The bottom section folds up over the top section.

Q10   D
The top section folds down over the bottom section.

Test 5

Q1   **A**

Q2   **B**

Q3   **A**

Q4   **A**

Q5   **D**

Q6   **B**

Q7   **B**

Q8   **D**

Q9   **B**

Q10   **C**

Test 6

Q1   **B**
The shape has 9 blocks visible from above, which rules out A, C and D.

Q2   **D**
The shape has 6 blocks visible from above, which rules out B and C. The shape only has 1 horizontal line of 3 blocks, which rules out A.

Q3   **C**
The shape only has 1 block in the centre of the front row, which rules out A, B and D.

Q4   **A**
The shape has a hole surrounded by blocks, which rules out B, C and D.

Q5   **B**
The shape has 7 blocks visible from above, which rules out A, C and D.

Q6   **B**
The shape has 8 blocks visible from above, which rules out A and C. The shape has 1 dark block visible from above, which rules out D.

Q7   **A**
The shape has no dark blocks visible from above, which rules out B, C and D.

Q8   **A**
The shape has 1 dark block visible from above, which rules out D. The dark block is in the back row of the shape with a light block to its left, which rules out B and C.

Q9   **D**
The shape has 5 blocks visible from above, which rules out A and C. The shape has no dark blocks visible from above, which rules out B.

Q10   **B**
The shape has 2 dark blocks visible from above, which rules out A, C and D.

Test 7

Q1   **A**
There is a horizontal block 2 cubes wide at the top of the shape when viewed from the top. This rules out B, C and D.

Q2   **C**
When viewed from the top, a square face of a cuboid is closest to the viewer. This rules out B and D. The shape is 3 cubes wide when viewed from the top. This rules out A.

Q3   **D**
There is a horizontal block 3 cubes wide at the top of the shape when viewed from the top. This rules out A, B and C.

Q4   **C**
When viewed from the top, the top row is 3 cubes wide. This rules out A, B and D.

Q5   **C**
When viewed from the top, there is 1 cube in the top row. This rules out A, B and D.

Q6   **B**
When viewed from the top, a rectangular face of a cuboid is closest to the viewer. This rules out A and C. There is a block missing from the right-hand column when viewed from the top. This rules out D.

Q7   **B**
When viewed from the top, there is a column 3 cubes high at the back on the right. This rules out A, C and D.

Q8   **D**
When viewed from the top, a square face and a rectangular face are closest to the viewer. This rules out A, B and C.

Q9   **C**
When viewed from the top, there is 1 cube in the bottom layer. This rules out A, B and D.

Q10   **B**
When viewed from the top, a face with a surface area equivalent to 3 square faces is closest to the viewer. This rules out A, C and D.

Test 8

Q1   **D**

Q2   **A**

Q3 B

Q4 B

Q5 A

Q6 D

Q7 B

Q8 B

Q9 A

Q10 A

Test 9

Q1 A

Q2 B

Q3 C

Q4 C

Q5 B

Q6 D

Q7 C

Q8 A

Test 10

Q1 C

The largest faces of the shape are white, which rules out A and D. The smaller faces of the shape are not white, which rules out B.

Q2 D

The curved part of the shape is white, which rules out B and C. Neither circular face is dark grey, which rules out A.

Q3 A

The smaller rectangular faces of the shape are white, which rules out C and D. The larger faces are light grey, which rules out B.

Q4 C

The rectangular faces of the shape are all white, which rules out A, B and D.

Q5 A

The shape has no dark grey triangular sides, which rules out B and C. The shape only has 1 light grey triangular side, which rules out D.

Q6 D

The shape has 1 dark grey face, which rules out A. The shape has no light grey sides, which rules out B and C.

Q7 A

The largest faces of the shape are both white, which rules out B, C and D.

Q8 C

The triangular faces of the shape are dark grey, which rules out A and B. None of the rectangular faces of the shape is dark grey, which rules out D.

Q9 A

The rectangular faces of the shape are all white, which rules out B, C and D.

Q10 D

The shape does not have 2 grey trapezium-shaped sides next to each other, which rules out A and B. The shape does not have 2 white trapezium-shaped sides next to each other, which rules out C.

Test 11

Q1 A

Q2 C

Q3 B

Q4 C

Q5 D

Q6 A

Q7 B

Q8 C

Q9 D

Q10 A

Test 12

Q1 C

Q2 D

Q3 C

Q4 B

Q5 B

Q6 B

Q7 C

Q8 D

Q9 C

Q10 C

Test 13

Q1 A

Q2 B

Q3 D

Q4 A

Q5 B

Q6 C

Q7 D

Q8 A

Q9 A

Q10 A

Q11 C

Q12 B

Test 14

Q1 B

Q2 B

Q3 A

Q4 B

Q5 B

Q6 C

Q7 B

Q8 D

Q9 A

Q10 C

Test 15

Q1 F
A 90° horizontal rotation clockwise.

Q2 B
A 180° vertical rotation.

Q3 C
A 90° vertical rotation forwards.

Q4 D
A 90° horizontal rotation anticlockwise.

Q5 A
A 180° horizontal rotation.

Q6 B
A 90° vertical rotation backwards. A 180° horizontal rotation.

Q7 D
A 90° horizontal rotation clockwise. A 90° vertical rotation backwards.

Q8 E
A 90° vertical rotation backwards.

Q9 A
A 90° horizontal rotation anticlockwise. A 90° vertical rotation backwards.

Q10 C
A 90° vertical rotation backwards. A 90° horizontal rotation anticlockwise.

Q11 E
A 90° vertical rotation forwards. A 90° horizontal rotation clockwise.

Q12 F
A 180° vertical rotation. A 90° horizontal rotation anticlockwise.

Test 16

Q1 A
The right section folds over the left section.

Q2 D
The top section folds over the bottom section.

Q3 B
The top section folds over the bottom section.

Q4 A
The right section folds over the left section.

Q5 D
The left section folds over the right section.

Q6 A
The left section folds over the right section.

Q7 C
The left section folds over the right section.

Q8 C
The bottom section folds over the top section.

Q9 D
The bottom section folds over the top section.

Q10 B
The bottom section folds over the top section.

Test 17

Q1 C

Q2 B

Q3 D

Q4 D

Q5   **C**

Q6   **A**

Q7   **D**

Q8   **B**

Q9   **D**

Q10   **A**

Test 18

Q1   **C**

The shape has 6 blocks visible from the right, which rules out A, B and D.

Q2   **C**

The shape has 8 blocks visible from the right, which rules out B and D. There is a block missing in the top left when viewing from the right, which rules out A.

Q3   **A**

There are 4 blocks visible from the right, which rules out B, C and D.

Q4   **B**

There are 4 blocks visible from the right, which rules out C and D. When viewing from the right, there is a vertical column of 3 blocks, which rules out A.

Q5   **D**

There are 6 blocks visible from the right, which rules out A, B and C.

Q6   **A**

There are 2 dark blocks visible from the right, which rules out B and D. When viewing from the right, there is 1 dark block on the left side of the middle row, which rules out C.

Q7   **A**

There is 1 dark block visible from the right, which rules out B, C and D.

Q8   **D**

There are no dark blocks visible from the right, which rules out A, B and C.

Q9   **C**

There are 5 blocks visible from the right, which rules out D. There is 1 dark block visible from the right, which rules out B. When viewing from the right, the dark block is on the left-hand side, which rules out A.

Q10   **D**

There are no dark blocks visible from the right, which rules out A, B and C.

Test 19

Q1   **B**

When viewed from the back, there is a column 2 cubes high on the right. This rules out A, C and D.

Q2   **D**

When viewed from the back, there is a square face on the top left. This rules out, A, B and C.

Q3   **C**

When viewed from the back, there is a column 3 cubes high closest to the viewer, without a cube to its right. This rules out A, B and D.

Q4   **D**

When viewed from the back, there is a column 3 cubes high in the middle. This rules out A, B and C.

Q5   **C**

When viewed from the back, there is a square face in the bottom left. This rules out A, B and D.

Q6   **C**

When viewed from the back, there is a square face in the bottom right. This rules out A, B and D.

Q7   **B**

When viewed from the back, there is a rectangular face 3 cubes wide. This rules out A, C and D.

Q8   **C**

When viewed from the back, there is a square face in the middle on the right. This rules out A, B and D.

Q9   **A**

When viewed from the back, there is a column 3 cubes high. This rules out B, C and D.

Q10   **A**

When viewed from the back, there is a rectangular face 2 cubes wide on the top with no other faces to its left or right. This rules out B, C and D.

Test 20

Q1   **D**

Q2   **A**

Q3   **B**

Q4   **B**

Q5   **D**

Q6   **B**

Q7   **C**

Q8   **A**

Q9   **C**

Q10   **A**

Test 21

Q1   B

Q2   D

Q3   A

Q4   A

Q5   B

Q6   A

Q7   D

Q8   B

Test 22

Q1   B

The curved face of the shape has horizontal stripes, which rules out A, C and D.

Q2   A

The rectangular faces either side of the upper grey face of the shape are both dark grey, which rules out C and D. The largest faces of the shape are both light grey, which rules out B.

Q3   C

The hexagonal faces are both white, which rules out D. The shape has 2 dark grey square faces which are next to each other, which rules out A and B.

Q4   B

The shape has only 1 dark grey face, which rules out A. This face is one of the smallest on the shape, which rules out D. The small face next to the dark grey face is white, which rules out C.

Q5   D

The square faces of the shape are all white, which rules out A, B and C.

Q6   D

The 3 shorter rectangular faces are all light grey, which rules out A, B and C.

Q7   A

The shape has 1 light grey and 1 dark grey face, which rules out B and C. The shape has no striped face, which rules out D.

Q8   C

The shape's triangular grey faces are not adjacent, which rules out B and D. The shape's triangular white faces are not adjacent, which rules out A.

Q9   A

The shape's 2 trapezium-shaped faces are both dark grey, which rules out D. The smallest face is dark grey, which rules out B. None of the rectangular shaped faces is dark grey, which rules out C.

Q10   C

The shape has only 1 dark grey triangular face, which rules out A. The light grey triangular faces are to the left of the dark grey triangular face, which rules out B. The white triangular face is to the left of the light grey triangular faces, which rules out D.

Test 23

Q1   A

Q2   C

Q3   B

Q4   C

Q5   D

Q6   A

Q7   B

Q8   C

Q9   D

Q10   A

Test 24

Q1   B

Q2   C

Q3   D

Q4   B

Q5   C

Q6   C

Q7   B

Q8   A

Q9   D

Q10   D

Test 25

Q1   C

When viewing from the back, the shape has a column of 3 blocks on its right-hand side, which rules out A, B and D.

Q2   B

The shape has 4 blocks visible from the back, which rules out A, C and D.

Q3   C

The shape has 8 blocks visible from the back, which rules out A, B and D.

Q4   A

The shape has 9 blocks visible from the back, which rules out B, C and D.

Q5   D

The shape has 5 blocks visible from the back, which rules out B and C. When viewing from the back, the shape has a column of 3 blocks on its left-hand side, which rules out A.

Q6   C

The shape has 7 blocks visible from the back, which rules out B and D. When viewing from the back, the shape has a horizontal row of 3 blocks at the bottom, which rules out A.

Q7   A

The shape has no dark blocks visible from the back, which rules out C and D. When viewing from the back, the shape has 1 block in the top row, which rules out B.

Q8   B

The shape has 6 blocks visible from the back, which rules out A, C and D.

Q9   D

The shape has no dark blocks visible from the back, which rules out A, B and C.

Q10   D

The shape has 2 dark blocks visible from the back, which rules out A. When viewing from the back, the shape has a column of 3 blocks on the right that consists of 1 dark block on top of 2 light blocks. This rules out B and C.

Notes

Notes

Notes